P9-DMR-856

Banff Town Warden

The Journals of Walter H. Peyto
Rocky Mountains Park, Banff
1914 to 1922

Edited by David W. Peyto

To Danny

Peyto Lake Books

Front cover picture: Walter Peyto (left) and Charlie Phillips
with the fire pump outfit on pack horses in 1920. Courtesy
Whyte Museum of the Canadian Rockies. V573 NA66-2177.

All rights reserved. No part of this work may be reproduced or
transmitted in any form or by any means, electronic or
mechanical, including photocopying and recording, or by any
information storage or retrieval system, except as may be
expressly permitted in writing from the publisher.

Printed and bound in Canada by
Blitzprint, Calgary.

Published by
Peyto Lake Books
59, 3302 - 50th St. N.W.
Calgary, Alberta T3A 2C6

Copyright 2002 - David W. Peyto
2nd Printing 2003

National Library of Canada Cataloguing in Publication Data

Peyto, Walter H., 1883-1963
    Banff town warden : the journals of Walter H. Peyto, Rocky
Mountains Park, Banff, 1914 to 1922 / edited by David W. Peyto

ISBN 0-9731066-0-3

    1. Peyto, Walter H., 1883-1963. 2. Banff National Park
(Alta.)--History. 3. Park rangers--Alberta--Banff National Park--
Biography. I. Peyto, David W II. Title.

FC3664.B3P49 2002   971.23'3202'092   C2002-902506-0
F1079.B5P49 2002

This book is dedicated to the memory of my grandparents:
Walter H. and Rosabelle Peyto and their children - Walter A.,
Stan, Syd, Edith, Harold and Helen.

email: dwpeyto@telus.net
web: www.peytolakebooks.com

Acknowledgements

I wish to thank several people who gave me assistance during the preparation of the material for this book.

I greatly appreciate the efforts of Don Bourdon and Lena Goon and other staff members of the Whyte Museum of the Canadian Rockies in Banff who provided excellent assistance in locating material in the archives relative to my grandfather's journals.

Thank you to Craig Richards and the Whyte Museum Archives staff for their excellent work on the reproduction of the archives' photographs included in this book.

I would like to acknowledge the late Henry Ness of Banff who spent a great amount of time talking to me about early Banff and some of the people mentioned in the journals. I also wish to acknowledge the late Maryalice Stewart who spent time talking with Henry and me.

Thank you to Gordon Burles of Banff for reviewing the manuscript and for the interest he has shown in the journals.

I would like to thank my sisters, Margaret Peyto and Carol Cole, my brother-in-law, Ron Cole and my nephews and niece (Andrew, Ethan, Tim and Yolande Cole) for taking the time to review the manuscript and for the interest they have shown in my editing of our grandfather's journals.

Thank you to Martha Root for the use of her photo of Billy Carver's cabin near Johnson Lake which appears on the back cover.

Thank you to Errol Smith for drawing the maps.

Thank you to my cousins, Joy Glenn and Shirley Cockerton, for lending me their family photo albums.

Thank you to Ted Hart of the Whyte Museum for his comments and assistance.

Thank you to Jon Whelan of Banff for his support during my visits to the Whyte Museum archives.

Thank you also to friends who have expressed an interest in this project.

Table of Contents

Introduction to Banff Town Warden

This book is based on the journals written by my grandfather, Walter H. Peyto (pronounced Pea-toe). The journals detail his experiences as the District One Fire and Game Warden in Rocky Mountains Park, which later became Banff National Park.

Walter was born in 1883 in Welling, Kent, England, the second youngest of nine children. He arrived in the Banff area in 1902, following in the footsteps of his older brother Bill, who came to Canada in 1887, and after whom Peyto Lake is named. Another older brother, Stephen and his family, lived in the Anthracite area just east of Banff for many years.

Walter started working in the Banff area by assisting Bill with his guiding and pack horse business. In the winters, Walter worked as a labourer for the Dominion Government for two dollars per ten hour day. For two summers, he ran the first tourist saddle horse business for the CPR up to the Sulphur Mountain Observatory.

After the Brewsters bought the transportation business from the railway, Walter drove for Dr. R.G. Brett who operated the Sanitarium Hotel, which was located on the site of the present day Administration Building at the south end of the Bow River Bridge in Banff. Walter also drove for the King Edward Hotel.

After one winter as a government teamster, Walter was appointed District One Fire and Game Warden in 1914. The warden for this district operated out of Banff. Walter worked for the Warden Service for 34 continuous years before retiring in 1948. For many years in retirement, he worked as a night guard if the RCMP had prisoners.

In 1902, Walter met his future wife, Rosabelle Hay, who had come to Banff from Alexandria, Ontario, that same year to work at the Banff Springs Hotel. They married in 1910 and made their home at 433 Banff Avenue, where they raised their family of six children, Walter A., Stanley, Sydney, Edith, Harold and Helen.

Walter and Rosabelle continued to live in Banff after his retirement. He died in Banff in 1963. Rosabelle died in Calgary in 1965 at the age of 88.

The Journals

As a park warden, Walter was required to keep brief, daily records of his official duties. These diaries were then submitted to the government in Ottawa. This book contains a selection of journal entries from Walter's own personal journals which show the wide variety of Walter's duties and responsibilities. The journal entries have been kept in his own words as much as possible, while making minor corrections with spelling and grammar. Some of the work duty descriptions may seem rather harsh and environmentally extreme for a national park warden based on today's standards. The exclusion of such incidents and descriptions from this book would not have given an accurate account of the life of these early wardens.

This book covers the earliest years of the journals. Some information has been added about people, events and places mentioned in the journals. Articles from The Banff Crag & Canyon newspaper which relate to journal entries are included in the book.

Most of the journal entries which mentioned someone by name are included. The Banff Crag & Canyon was researched in the preparation of biographies for many of these people. If someone was only mentioned once or twice and/or there was difficulty in obtaining information, there may not be a biography. Variations in spelling were found for some individuals during the research. I apologize to their descendents for any spelling mistakes. Sometimes only a last name was mentioned in the journals. If more than one person of that surname was in the Banff area at the time, biographies for all the individuals with that surname are included.

In reading the journals, it can be seen that Walter's work

involved long hours, few days off and a wide variety of duties.

He had to check on fires in and around Banff, sometimes being called out in the middle of the night. These fires may have been caused by picnic groups or campers, by hobos who got off a train, or by a passing train. There were sometimes problems controlling fires that started in and around the Garbage Grounds or Dump (also called the Nuisance Grounds) which was located across the Spray River Bridge near the Golf Course (Golf Links). Walter's duties also involved the maintenance and care of the fire pumps and hoses. Sometimes he worked on posting fire notices for local residents and visitors.

Another duty was the installation and maintenance of telephone lines in the Banff area.

Walter had many duties involving animals. As per the park policy of that era, he and other wardens were expected to control the predators such as coyotes or crows which were seen as a threat to other animals and birds. He was called upon to investigate conflicts between bears and local residents and/or visitors. This may have involved scaring the bear away or having to shoot the more aggressive bears.

He had to check on reports of wounded or dead animals, such as deer and elk, in and around Banff. These injuries or deaths were often caused by trains or cars. He also had to deal with wild animals being attacked or threatened by local dogs. As this problem became more serious, he was expected to capture or shoot the dogs. When cats running loose became a nuisance, he was expected to solve this problem. Local residents not wanting to keep their dogs or cats often called upon Walter to destroy the animals.

He also had the job of helping to supply food for the meat-eating animals in the Banff Zoo. This meat might have come from wild animals that had been seriously wounded or killed or from killing old horses.

The National Parks also had a policy of shipping wild animals from the park to other parts of Canada, the United States or overseas. Walter was involved with the capture and shipping of these animals. A few times he took extended trips outside the park accompanying these animals on the train.

Walter's job also consisted of patrolling in and around Banff checking for fishing violations, sealing firearms, and watching for poachers.

As the wardens' use of vehicles increased, his duties included the maintenance of these vehicles. He also transported materials and men for jobs such as road and trail gangs, fire crews, picnic and camp ground work crews, and brush burning crews.

If people were missing or lost he was called upon to help in the search. Sometimes this involved walking or riding the trails at night.

From time to time he had other duties such as helping with mosquito control, taking coal up to the Sulphur Mountain Observatory by horse, driving park dignitaries or special visitors around the Banff area, or accompanying film crews to different locations.

I hope this book will give the reader a better understanding of the difficult and demanding work undertaken by these early park wardens.

The Early Warden Patrols in Rocky Mountains Park

The Fire and Game Guardian Service in the park was started in 1909 with the hiring of the first Chief Game Guardian, Howard Sibbald. That summer, Banff residents John Hogarth and Robert Robertson were hired as game guardians. Robertson spent three years on the job while Hogarth stayed only a short time.

In the winter of 1910, there were seven temporary game guardians. Three additional men, Walker, Fay and Knott, were sworn in as game guardians in 1911.

In the spring of 1913, Sibbald was looking to expand the Warden Service to twelve from five. Some of the wardens during 1913 included Jack Bevan, E.W. (Bill) Peyto, William Noble, Edward Tabuteau, Ben Woodworth, Howard Caine, Andrew (Scotty) Wright, Burton S. Fox, Louis Hill, John McKay, William George Fyfe, Thomas Staple, L.S. Mumford and L.A. Mill. Eight of these men continued to work that winter: Fyfe at Castle Mountain, Peyto and Mumford at Banff, Caine at Laggan, Bevan and Noble at Canmore, Staple at Exshaw and Wright at Bankhead. In 1914, Walter Peyto, J.F. Morrison, Fred Ashley and John Joseph Leitcher were added to the warden patrol in Rocky Mountains Park.

Walter Peyto driving for the Sanitarium Hotel in 1905. Bob Lothian is standing beside the coach. Whyte Museum of the Canadian Rockies. V484 NA 66-2074.

Goats at Banff Animal Paddock. Whyte Museum of the
Canadian Rockies. V573 NA66-2398.

Cars and Tally Ho at Bow River Bridge. Whyte Museum of the
Canadian Rockies. V573 NA66-480.

Peyto family home at 433 Banff Avenue

Moose at Animal Paddock.

The Journals - Nineteen Fourteen

June 1914

June 8th - Cloudy, some rain (cool)
Went to Buffalo Park to catch two horses for Fyfe, to Whiskey Creek and rode river and then up track and along the river - posting signs, 8 miles rode.

June 10th - Cloudy, some rain
Went to Anthracite to see what old shacks are standing yet and to burn up old outhouse, also posted up fire signs, rode 10 miles.

June 11th - Fine
Hot Springs, CPR Hotel, Middle Springs, Loop, down to Bow as far as big eddy, also posted signs, walked along upper end of Whiskey Creek through moose pasture looking for stray fishermen, rode 12 miles.

June 12th - Fine
Along west side of Tunnel Mountain then down to Loop to get sign board from Indian House pits and placed sign at pits on west side of Tunnel Mountain, rode and walked along Whiskey and Echo Creeks, 14 miles walked and rode.

June 15th - Hot
Up Tunnel Mountain Road by falls, around bush near station looking for camp fires left by hobos, found new remains of two deer, one on Tunnel and one in bush near station, both apparently died a natural death, rode 10 miles.

June 18th - Fine, hot
Fighting fire at Devil's Lake opposite Game Warden's cabin, fire caused by lightning, wind from east starting up old brush fire, remains in moss under control, came back in afternoon, burned about 2 acres - small timber, small fire on Forty Mile Creek, no damage done - ¼ acre, willows suffering worst.

June 19th - Fine
Walked around timber at CPR Station looking for fires left by hobos, found two small ones, went to Hot Springs by wagon road and back by bridle path, to CPR Hotel, down to

Bow Falls, rode 7 miles.

June 22nd - Rain

Went to Loop to see fire at Garbage Grounds, notified men and stable foreman to have rubbish taken to bottom of hill to let fire in manure die down, also got word of a bear bothering people on Mountain Avenue, made inquiries, found out bear is a big brown, came on Sunday night to back verandah, stole strawberries, saw signs of him being at nearby places.

June 25th - Raining all day

Walked down to Buffalo Park and around by track to town, saw two men pass house that looked like they might be going fishing.

June 28th

Walked through moose pasture and west up track to mile board 83, discovered small fire in timber 75 feet from right of way, camp fire left by hobos, burning in moss, CPR Fire Warden helped put it out, no damage done, walked 5 miles.

June 30th - Hot

Travelled up Tunnel Mountain to near top and out at large tree lying across trail, watched roads leading out from town to see who was going fishing, met Mumford coming in from Spray Lakes with horses - very thin, rode 10 miles.

July 1914

July 1st - Fine

Rode to good fishing points and watched fishing parties did not exceed limit, water too high for really good fishing, rode 14 miles.

July 5th - Cloudy, thunderstorms

Saw Jack Ballard going west with saddle and 1 pack horse.

July 8th - Fine, hot

Through Mount Edith Pass, up Forty Mile Creek about 2 miles above 1st crossing with Cornell looking over trail, rode 10 miles.

July 9th - Hot

Hot Springs, then to lake, at Anthracite with Vick, 18 miles rode.

July 14ᵗʰ - Fine
Hunting for lost woman from 10:30 a.m. the time I first heard that woman was lost, J. Cornell with me, no trace.
July 15ᵗʰ - Showery
Looking for woman, to Anthracite and met Jack Cornell with horses, rode around with Sibbald to places where woman was said to have been seen.
July 16ᵗʰ - Hot
Hunting for woman in forenoon, woman found about 2:30.

The Banff Crag & Canyon - July 18ᵗʰ, 1914
Lost is Found - After 72 hours in the bush without food or shelter

After spending three days and three nights in the bush alongside the Bow River, between the cemetery and the falls, 72 hours without food and with no shelter from the weather but the branches of trees under which she made her bed on the ground, while hundreds of men scoured the woods and mountainsides for her, Mrs. Thos. Lees Finlayson was accidentally discovered and returned to her boarding house Thursday.

Mrs. Finlayson left the Shaw house on Marten Street, where she was boarding shortly after noon Monday. It had been her custom to take a walk every afternoon when feeling equal to the exertion, but failing to return to the house by supper time a search was instituted. Later on in the evening the police were notified of the woman's disappearance and the search continued until darkness intervened.

Tuesday morning the search was resumed, the entire police force of six men augmented by parties of citizen volunteers spending the major portion of the day riding and walking through the underbrush surrounding the town.

About ten o'clock Tuesday morning Dr. Learn notified Supt. Clarke of the woman's disappearance and 14 government men were ordered to assist in the search. They spent the balance of the day in an effort to find some trace of her, then abandoned further search on the theory that her body was in the river.

The search was continued all day Wednesday, some parties going down the river, others in different directions.

16

Numerous parties not stimulated by thought of reward but in the cause of humanity were out all Thursday forenoon but it was only by the merest accident that she was discovered.

Robert Daniel was walking along the river bank and in taking a short cut up to the road almost stepped upon the lost woman, lying under a tree.

July 17th - Fine
At Buffalo Park helping Woodworth round up buffalo and moving horses to new pasture, fixing gate at new pasture.
July 18th - Hot
To Captain Grey's camp at Massive and Phillips' camp, saw old black bear at Sawback, rode 22 miles.
July 20th - Cloudy (snow on mountain)
To Observatory on Sulphur Mountain for Sanson and to Sundance Canyon to fire reported by tourist driver as big bush fire, no damage, apparently caused by cigar and out in open, rode 26 miles.
July 21st - Cloudy
Along Motor Road to Mount Edith, Buffalo Park, to Alpine Club House looking for bear in evening, reported at office that bear ripped side of tent where girls were sleeping, saw where he ripped the tent, 10 miles rode.
July 22nd - Cloudy
Building corral to catch horses in moose pasture, Hot Springs, falls and Alpine Club in evening, looking for bear, saw last year's cub, rode 15 miles.
July 30th - Hot
Smoke more noticeable today but not around Banff, Spray Valley to fire guard, located doe deer with leg off this evening, killed it, 16 miles.

August 1914
August 2nd - Hot
Very smoky all through valley, could not see mountains in early morning, a little cloudy later, smoke apparently coming from west, rode around woods near depot and to

basin to get high up.

August 3rd - Fine, warm

Up Sulphur Mountain with Miss Arnott of Ottawa to fix clocks for Sanson, 16 miles rode.

August 5th - Hot

From Banff to Red Earth Creek, met Carslake and two fellows working with him, fixed pack for them, horse rolled with saddle and got his foot through stirrup, saddle turned under and horse gave a good exhibition of bucking, 18 miles rode.

August 6th - Cloudy, some rain

Mouth of Red Earth Creek to Shadow Lake, came back 1 ½ miles to camp, 12 miles rode and walked, big thunderstorm during night.

August 7th - Cloudy and cold rain

Along east branch of Red Earth Creek, from Shadow Lake over summit to Healy Creek, 19 miles rode and walked, very cold crossing summit, some snow, packed up Sanson's camp (trail passable but not good).

August 12th - Fine

To second Eau Claire camp with Jack Cornell, fixed up goat traps, left Jack up at camp, saw Joe Boyce and party of three fishing, rode 10 miles.

August 15th - Hot, smoke in valley

Helped Sibbald pack up in forenoon and after dinner, agent at Bankhead notified office of fire up towards dam, started out to investigate, saw fire was over Squaw Mountain so sent timekeeper Holmes up to dam for gang of men to go up creek, fire started from smouldering rotten logs at camp of engineers, fire was seen smouldering by three men who poured water on it and thought they had it completely out, about 75 to 80 men fighting fire till morning.

August 16th - Cloudy, heavy rain at night

With Bill Peyto and two pack horses with grub for fire fighters, returned to town, left Bill up at fire.

August 19th - Fine and warm

About Banff in forenoon, to Spray Valley for goat in

afternoon, fire broke out fresh about noon, Sibbald and McAulay took out bunch of men, 18 miles rode.

August 20th - Fine, showery in evening

Through Mount Edith Pass as far as Forty Mile Creek, took John McKay out to cut trail to fire fighters' camp on Squaw in evening, met George Luxton and two others riding through Mount Edith Pass, 18 miles rode.

August 24th - Fine

Up Stoney Squaw Mountain to fire camp, to Hot Springs in afternoon, met Fred Gladwin with party of 1 man and 2 ladies including Mrs. and Dr. Harry Brett, doctor to follow 5 pack horses heading north, rode 14 miles.

August 31st - Fine

Mount Edith Pass to J. McKay's camp, then on up creek to locate place for G.W. (Game Warden) cabin, also took out supplies for John, 20 miles rode.

September 1914

September 4th - Dull, some rain

To Buffalo Park to see Ben about yak, up Squaw Mountain in afternoon, 12 miles rode.

September 7th - Cloudy and cold, rain afternoon and evening

To Buffalo Park cutting yak's teeth with Howard and Mr. Courtice, 4 or 5 miles rode and walked.

September 8th - Cold, rain, fair in afternoon

To Spray River logging camp, L. Randall reported three goats in trap, went up but gate was open, 20 miles rode.

September 9th - Cloudy, rain in forenoon

Drove team out to Lake Minnewanka with camp outfit for J. McKay and Ashley, 16 miles rode.

September 10th - Cloudy

Packed in tools and camp outfit from Squaw Mountain, met two fellows looking for Forty Mile Creek, rained all night, 8 miles rode.

September 16th - Cloudy, stormy in afternoon, heavy rain at night

To Buffalo Park to catch horse for Courtice and to Healy Creek in afternoon with H. Sibbald locating places for cabins and blazing trail leading from river to cabin site to bring along timber, 14 miles rode, saw Harrison and Jack Dawson coming to Banff from Simpson Summit.

September 19th - Rain, cool

To Spray Valley to look at bear traps, west as far as Eau Claire camp, saw 12 goats and 1 black bear cub, met H. Gordon fishing, 32 miles rode.

September 21st - Cloudy, cool

To trap up Spray Valley, tracked bear for about 6 miles, met 6 tourists about 3 miles up road where mud was very thick, turned back, 16 miles rode.

September 23rd - Fine and warm

Hauled material for cabin with camp outfit of J. McKay and Fred Ashley to Massive, saw J. Brewster and J. Lowry riding west, 22 miles rode.

September 25th - Fine and warm

To pasture for horses and Sundance Canyon in afternoon, J. Warren went north looking for hunters and to put other boys wise that men were in that district, 12 miles rode.

September 28th - Fine, warm

To Spray Valley and Sundance Creek, saw Fred and Jack Ballard going south with pack outfit, sealed rifle for each one, 22 miles rode.

September 29th

Healy and Sundance, looking for wounded deer, about 15 miles rode and walked, sealed 2 rifles for Ben Fay - 1 Luger, 1 Winchester.

September 30th - Clear and windy

To Spray goat traps, coyotes had been around traps, shut traps up, to Anthracite to see what they were doing about tearing down old building, sealed 3 rifles for Harrison - 2 Mausers, 1 Winchester, 26 miles rode.

October 1914

October 1st - Cloudy, cold

To Massive to move cabin builders' camp to 7 miles west of Banff, saw young porcupine taking a swim in Bow River, rode out to Sundance Canyon looking for deer supposed to be lying dead beside road, sealed rifle for Tex Wood, drove 22 miles, rode 8 miles.

October 5th - Rain and snow

Around town, looking for stolen roofing, heard of man being killed today by bear at Spray Lakes, Sibbald leaving tonight for Canmore.

October 6th - Clear and warm

Cave and Basin Road, station, Golf Links, Sibbald phoned in from Spray Lakes for Unwin and I to go out tonight, we left about 8:30 p.m., arrived at cabin about 4:00 a.m., about 35 miles rode and walked.

October 7th - Snow and rain

Started out to look for grizzly with Unwin, Sibbald, Stearns and Mumford, found bear lying dead at Stearns' bog about 1 mile N.W. of camp (logging) in main Spray Valley, bear had 4 bullet holes in her and we also saw place where Lovgren was killed. I picked up his upper row of teeth and shreds of his scalp, bear not large and we could not see how the bear had been coming towards the man when he fired the four shots as three went in sideways and the other in near the tail, Lovgren lost his life no doubt on account of the cartridge missing fire, 30.85 size of rifle, ammunition Dominion, noted too its missing fire.

The Banff Crag & Canyon - October 11th, 1914

Killed by Grizzly - A Young Swede Laborer Meets Death near the Spray Lakes

Oscar Lovgren, a young Swede was killed by a grizzly Monday afternoon near the Spray Lakes.

The news reached the town Monday evening and Howard Sibbald left for the scene of the killing Tuesday. The body was recovered and brought to Canmore, where Coroner Thomson held an inquest Wednesday.

The facts brought out at the inquest are as follows:

Lovgren who was only 24 years of age had been in Canada for about twelve months, was at the lumber camp near the Spray Lakes with a companion named Wilson waiting to be put to work, although not on the pay roll. Monday, Lovgren took a rifle, belonging to Gombart, one of the foremen, and went out to look for a bear that had been reported as being in the neighbourhood of the camp. He returned to the camp at noon and reported having found the bear and killed it, firing five shots into the bruin. After eating dinner, he with two companions went out to skin the bear and bring in the meat. When they arrived at the spot where he had "killed" the animal, the bear was not there, but a trail of blood disclosed its whereabouts and the three hunters confidently approached the wounded beast without using precautions to ascertain if it were really and truly dead.

Lovgren, who was carrying the rifle, was slightly in the rear of his two companions when with a blood-curdling roar the wounded grizzly rose to her feet and ignoring the two men in front, made straight for the man with the gun. Lovgren had no time to shoot and with one sweep of her mighty paw the man's face was torn off and his skull crushed to jelly. The other two men lost no time in making their get-away and reaching the camp gave the alarm.

When Sibbald arrived at the scene of the killing, which is reached by pack trail through White Man's Pass, he found the bear, a female grizzly, stone dead about 300 yards from where Lovgren had been killed. The carcass contained five bullets.

The jury returned a verdict of accidental death. Sgt. Oliver of the RNWMP Canmore laid an information against Gombart for having in his possession an unsealed rifle within the limits of the Rocky Mountains Park and F.W. Knott, J.P. disposed of the case by imposing a fine of $25.00 and costs.

October 16th - Clear and windy
To Observatory on Sulphur Mountain with four pack horses - coal and supplies for Sanson, snow started when on the mountain, heavy rain when I got to Hot Springs - 4 a.m., rode 10 miles.

October 19th - Clear, cold (heavy frost at night)
Anthracite and Duthil with Jack Warren, tried German

ammunition, 5 missed out of 5, 15 miles rode.

October 21st - Cloudy and warm, heavy frost at night
To Devil's Lake to help Scotty move, 16 miles rode.

October 22nd - Clear and warm after sun got up
To Bankhead helping Scotty Wright build up his shack, got Ballard to fix rifle sight at night, 10 miles rode.

October 23rd - Clear and warm
Fixing gasoline engine on Sibbald's car forenoon, took a long ride back of Recreation Grounds after coyote, along Basin Creek, 5 or 6 miles rode, met Mrs. Ashton - she told me she had seen a mountain lion at the spring, phoned W. Garrett but he had not seen it.

October 24th - Clear, warm
To Hot Springs by bridle path and back by road looking for sign of mountain lion, stayed at Hot Springs all forenoon, to Healy Creek afternoon with grub, 14 miles rode.

November 1914

November 3rd - Clear, 4 inches of snow last night
Gathering up horses and branding them before they go to Red Deer for winter with Howard Caine.

November 4th - Snow, storming all day
Lots of deer came in close last night.

November 5th - Snowing from N.E.
Rounded up horses in pasture and went with Sibbald and Wright to Canmore, 32 miles rode, blowing a blizzard all the way.

November 21st - Clear
Squaw Mountain, Motor Road to Third Lake, Loop, Howard sent me to Brewster's store to seal five rifles that were in their window, rode 11 miles.

November 23rd - Fine
Up Forty Mile Creek to dam, to Third Lake forenoon, 12 miles rode, Leversage brought doe deer from Anthracite - had been hurt on tracks - Sibbald killed it.

November 28th - Clear
Along foot of Squaw Mountain and sloughs east of Moffatt

Milk Ranch, walked to Sundance and Cave and Basin, walked 3 miles and rode 8 miles, saw two large buck deer in my yard this evening, very bold, one tried to stand me off.

December 1914

December 16th - Clear, cold
Middle Springs, Squaw Mountain, across sheep range to Tote Road, only saw 4 deer on mountain, went to Bankhead with Wright at night, stayed at Cascade House, paid $1.00 bed and breakfast.

December 17th - Clear, cold
From Bankhead to Ghost River Cabin by Devil's Lake to try and head off Harrison, 23 miles walked and carried pack, got to shack and found roofing all blown off, put in one awful night, had to keep stove red hot, got no sleep.

December 18th - Clear, cold
Along Ghost River to Devil's Head Mountain trying to pick up tracks of Harrison and Latimer, no sign whatever, Jonas Two Young Men came to cabin around 2 a.m., he came over trail from Morley, he saw no tracks so we decided to pull for Banff in the morning, 15 miles walked.

December 19th - Clear, warmer
From Ghost River Cabin to Banff by Devil's Lake, 22 miles walked, got to Banff after dark, saw where deer had been killed at east end of lake, nothing but hair and insides left, only animal tracks, cougar supposed to be in that country.

December 20th - Clear, cold west wind
Sunday, took a rest, saw Sibbald and he said he had got our men last night after chasing them for two days.

December 22nd - Clear
Went up Forty Mile Creek past dam looking for trail of two men that went up creek on Sunday, supposed to be going for fish but were scared off by McAulay working at dam, nothing doing, went to Bankhead with rig and brought in pack outfit and Ballard who had been with Wright looking for evidence on Harrison on Stony Creek, they found meat packed in Stony Creek Cabin, 16 miles walked, rode and drove.

December 23rd - Clear

Getting marten ready and shipping to Seton Ltd., Connecticut, USA, to Loop in afternoon and Spray River, flood is very high, road east of bridge is flooded for 100 yards, 6 or 7 miles rode.

December 28th - Clear

Hot Springs by bridle path and along Motor Road to sulphur spring, 27 sheep in one bunch at springs, very tame, within 10 feet of saddle horse and licking salt and did not scare when I walked towards them, an old ewe with horns off like she had been dehorned, 13 miles rode.

December 31st - Clear

Moose pasture, Vermilion Lakes to Bow River, down river to Banff, 10 miles rode, went to Healy Creek Cabin with the speeder on track after supper - to look for tracks on summit trail - moonlight, light as day, got home 1 a.m., 10 miles by speeder.

Bill Peyto at Simpson Summit cabin (1913). Whyte Museum of the Canadian Rockies. V573 NA66-262.

Nineteen Fifteen

January 1915
January 2nd - Cloudy
Along track to 2nd Lake and across Bow to Recreation Grounds and down to moose pasture with Mumford in afternoon, 5 or 6 miles walked.
January 4th - Snow forenoon, clear afternoon
Down around Moffatt's and to Sundance Canyon to shack of woodcutters, 12 miles rode and walked.
January 6th - Clear
Up valley west of Cascade Mountain, over Squaw Mountain, about 15 miles walked, sealed up gun for T. Frayne - Savage 303.
January 23rd - Cloudy, warmer
To Healy Creek Cabin, 12 miles snowshoes, met B. Noble, T. Frayne and one other on their way to Simpson River, B.C. to get outfit left by Graves and Gardiner.
January 29th - Clear
Motor Road to Lakes, Recreation Grounds and Loop, 10 miles walked, out after supper setting traps for coyotes on Forty Mile Creek.
January 30th - Clear, cold
Squaw Mountain, meadow on Basin Road and Hot Springs, out till 11 p.m. after coyotes, 10 miles walked and rode.

February 1915
February 2nd - Cloudy, warmer
No luck with traps, Motor Road, Forty Mile Creek, Tunnel Mountain, 7 or 8 miles walked and rode, inspected deer found dead for B. Woodworth.
February 3rd - Cloudy, snow forenoon, bright warm afternoon
Hot Springs and Motor Road, Forty Mile Creek, saw 1 coyote at daybreak, 10 or 12 miles rode, saw guests of Hot Springs Hotel trying to outrun a coyote in the bush - I having come to Hot Springs to try and get same coyote but

26

had ride for nothing.

February 7th - Clear and warm

Squaw Mountain and Moffatt's Ranch, 3 or 4 miles walked, shot 1 coyote last night, nothing in traps but lots of tracks around all traps, going to quit night hunting till coyotes get bolder and new moon comes.

February 9th

Up to office to report to Mr. Sibbald on Anthracite, notified Dofny to remove lumber from lot in Anthracite - forenoon, went to Anthracite with Sibbald and burnt up several shacks, 18 miles rode and drove.

February 11th - Clear, warm

Vermilion Lakes and Motor Road in forenoon, went to Canmore in afternoon with Mr. Sibbald on speeder, 20 miles rode and speeder.

February 17th - Colder

Buffalo Park and down by Moffatt's looking at traps set around carcass of deer taken from park, Tunnel Mountain Road, 10 miles rode.

February 20th - Colder forenoon, warmer afternoon

Out looking at traps forenoon, too sick to go out in afternoon - sick headaches, 5 miles rode.

February 22nd - Clear, warm after sun up

Loop and Sundance Canyon, 12 miles rode, coyotes getting shy - breeding.

February 24th - Cloudy

Out to traps forenoon and fixing speeder, down to station in afternoon setting traps sprung by owl, caught large horned owl in coyote trap, took same to Zoo, 2 miles rode.

March 1915

March 1st - Cold wind, warmer middle of day

Up Spray Valley with McMullen and to Sundance Canyon and Healy Creek trail, 14 miles rode.

March 4th - Clear, warm

Down by station looking at traps and to Buffalo Park, went up into bush west of Sanitarium Hotel to show Ballard where timber was to be burned, then went to Middle Springs and Hot Springs, 8 or 9 miles rode.

March 5th - Clear, warm

To Lakes, Middle Springs and along Hoodoos to mouth of Cascade River, found remains of deer caught in ice, baited carcass for coyotes, saw several deer and got 1 coyote, 14 miles rode.

March 6th - Clear, warm

Recreation Grounds, Cave and Basin and Motor Road to Sawback with Holmes, saw one lazy ram and about 25 sheep, saw several deer, 16 miles rode.

March 8th - Clear, warm

Along Tote Road to Forty Mile Creek and Hot Springs, in afternoon to Spray Valley, 14 miles rode, noticed several buck deer had shed their horns this week - are in town more just now.

March 10th - Clear, warm

To hills west of Anthracite looking at timber where Ashley and Axel were cutting, to Spray Valley in afternoon where Ballard is axe cutting for McMullen, 12 miles rode.

March 11th - Cloudy and some snow

Up to office with money for dog tax for Warden Wright, to station and Hot Springs with timekeeper Holmes in afternoon, saw no less than 11 persons between Hot Springs and Golf Links, must be sign of spring as 5 were ladies, 12 miles rode and walked.

March 15th - Dull, some rain

Motor Road, Spray Valley and along track 2 miles west burning outside right of way with section men and Mr. Sibbald, trying new torch, saw where campfire had been left in heavy timber - put same out, no damage, 7 or 8 miles rode.

March 16th - Dull, windy

To Hot Springs and Squaw Mountain and Tote Road, saw robin - first of season - up to office and reported having seen robin to Mr. Sanson, 10 miles rode and walked.

March 20th - Very warm

Loop and Cave and Basin and 3 miles west on speeder with Howard, saw 3 bluebirds and 1 crow, first I have seen this season, 9 miles rode.

March 24th - East wind, some snow

To Castle Mountain and back with H. Sibbald on speeder, had our own lunch at Fyfe's shack (his tea), looking for logs on Johnston Creek for shack at Massive, motor balked all the way home, reached home at 9 p.m., 30 miles on track.

March 27th - Dull, cold

Took motor to CPR Hotel engineer, getting camp outfit ready and loaded on wagon to take Mumford and McKay to Johnston Creek.

March 30th - Cloudy, warm

Banff to Johnston Creek by Motor Road with McKay's and Mumford's camp, home at 7 p.m., saw large number of sheep, 1 bunch of 13 had 9 rams altogether at salt lick (young), 28 miles drove.

April 1915

April 5th - Warm

To office and yard, Hot Springs in afternoon, found coyote shot two weeks ago with six shooter, got outfit and wagon ready to go to Johnston Creek in morning, 5 or 6 miles rode.

May 1915

May 11th - Fine

Buffalo Park and Massive, packing grub to camp at cabin, left three horses to pasture there, 25 miles rode, met L.J. Bushfield of Calgary looking for a grip that he had lost on Motor Road, Moffatt found grip, I shipped it to Eldon, I also met J. Boyce and another man riding to Massive.

May 12th - Fine, warm

To Golf Links and shot 15 gophers that are destroying greens, brought them to animal cages, loaded one load of lumber for Massive, 10 miles rode.

May 17th - Cloudy, cold

Hitched up roan horses, loaded material for Massive, left Banff at noon, got 2 ½ miles on Motor Road, small horse started kicking and ran up bank, dumped me out and I pulled them on line but wagon turned upside down onto lake shore taking horses with it, cleared horses of wagon and they went to middle of lake and then came out, got Maughton to give a hand and we finally got outfit - none the worse, sent word by Ray Bryden that I would not be up.

May 18th - Cloudy, cold

Packed two horses to Massive Cabin with cement and grub, 24 miles rode.

May 27th - Fine

Over Squaw to Cascade with Mr. Child to lay out trail, saw yearling black bear on way back, about 12 miles rode.

May 29th - Showery

Along new trail on Rundle Mountain to see Watrick to see how far he has trail done, to Anthracite in afternoon with Constable Shedden to investigate cause of house being set on fire, very few things saved, owner away, 10 or 11 miles rode.

June 1915

June 3rd - Fine

Got saddle horse shod forenoon, up Rundle Mountain to end of new trail to see Watrick, 5 or 6 miles rode, out in evening along creeks watching for fishermen, 2 miles walked.

June 4th - Fine till evening

Along Hot Springs Road and surrounding woods watching for black bear, 7 or 8 miles rode, bear had done some damage at Alpine Club and scared women.

June 5th - Fine forenoon, rain heavy afternoon

Patrolled from Cave and Basin to Hot Springs by Alpine Club and CPR Hotel till 10 p.m. looking for bear.

The Banff Crag & Canyon - June 5th, 1915

Alpine Club Might Close

A. O. Wheeler says unless the wild bears are driven from

the park the club will have no other option.

Mr. A. O. Wheeler, president of the Alpine Club of Canada, came to Banff last Sunday to superintend the opening of the Club House on the Upper Springs Road. Mr. Wheeler left early in the week making a short trip into the mountains and during his absence a big black bear visited the Club House during the wee hours of the morning and all but frightened the housekeeper into sickness.

His marks are very plain on the different window sills where he was inspecting the interior of the house. In another window he pulled the screen off, pushed in the sash and mixed up the housekeeper's food supplies. In another place he pulled down the water mains, breaking a 2 inch pipe and flooding the basement and caused untold damage. It is putting it mild to say that Mr. Wheeler is mad, and in an interview with him this morning he said, "Unless the park government destroy these bears at large, I will have no other option but to close the club house. Not only are they destructive, but I do not feel like taking the responsibility of the very lives of the members of this club. I tremble to think what might happen any time as these animals become more used to human beings. They become more dangerous. You remember several times last year several of our lady members were badly frightened by bears prowling around the tent. I am duty bound to take this complaint to the minister if nothing can be done in the Banff office."

The Banff Crag & Canyon - June 5[th,] 1915
Late Local News Notes

The bears around Banff are getting numerous and troublesome. Don Matheson's outhouses have been raided, Jack Ballard's camp near Sawback was pulled to pieces and the housekeeper in the Alpine Club House got the scare of her life last Thursday morning from a bear in the club house cellar.

June 6th - Rain showers, heavy rain set in about 9 p.m., rain fell till 7 p.m. June 7th.
Watching Hot Springs trail.
June 7th - Rain storms
Cave to Hot Springs forenoon looking for bear, Loop and

Garbage Grounds afternoon, 10 miles rode.

June 8th - Rain showers all day

Took John McKay to Forty Mile Creek first crossing via Mount Edith Pass, helped make camp, took horses to pasture on return, 15 miles rode.

June 9th - Fine forenoon, rain evening

To pasture for horses with Warden Bevan and helped Mumford and Curren get outfits ready forenoon, up Rundle Mountain locating more trail, found it almost impossible to get horse trail any higher without great expense, 9 miles rode, saw black bear on green patch on Squaw Mountain (from town).

June 10th - Showery

Up Cascade Trail by way of Squaw Mountain past Boyce's camp, got phone message from HES to go up and shoot bear, followed bear from Cave Avenue to Alpine Club, fixed two shots, possibly wounded bear but not having my dog could not get any track of bear up Sulphur Mountain, rode and walked.

June 11th - Showery

To pasture forenoon, helped Bevan, scouring side of Sulphur Mountain all afternoon for sign of bear - could not get any, rode and walked.

June 14th

To Rundle Mountain on new trail with HES and McMahon locating trail to peak, 8 or 9 miles rode and walked.

June 16th - Cloudy, rain 9:30 - evening

On lookout for horse, vet not here so turned horses out in pasture, on way to pasture met Warren, got him to lead two horses, the one that I led pulled his halter off and passed over one corner of Stewart lawn, out on Motor Road looking for stray horse, shot one coyote, got outfit ready for Mr. Sibbald, 10 miles rode.

June 22nd - Fine

Helped Curren pack up and went as far as CPR Hotel with him, Basin in afternoon, 5 miles rode.

June 24th - Fine forenoon, heavy thunderstorm afternoon
Working on motor pump forenoon, went moving Phillips' furniture to Massive Cabin in afternoon, 22 miles by motor velocipede.

June 25th - Rain
To pasture with Tex Wood for horses, up to Recreation Grounds for Phillips' string of horses, took them to pasture, helped Tex pack up in afternoon to go to Forty Mile Creek, 7 or 8 miles rode and walked, cleaning up motor, heavy rain set in about 5:30.

June 26th - Still rain at 6:30, rain all day
Helped McAulay pump out Stenton's cellar with gas pump, went to crossing of Forty Mile Creek via Mount Edith Pass accompanied by Warren and Tex Wood to try and get pack horses out that were drowned, creek running wild, could not get anything out, 15 miles rode.

June 27th - Fine
To Forty Mile Creek, got out one horse and caught some smaller things, John McKay helped, 15 miles rode, located white horse but could not get to him.

June 28th - Fine
To Forty Mile Creek and got white horse from creek and piled up for John McKay to burn.

July 1915
July 1st - Fine
Along creek and river to moose pasture, watching streams around Banff for fishermen with small fish, boys most trouble - wanting to keep undersized fish, down to pasture in afternoon for horses for vet to inspect, 12 miles rode and walked.

July 3rd - Fine
To Healy Creek Cabin with pack horses with Mr. Sibbald, caught Phillips' horses that came east while he was over river, 12 miles rode.

The Banff Crag & Canyon - July 3rd, 1915
Banff in Bad Flood

Citizens Watched Bow rise at rate of inch an hour for 36 hours

Banff, unlike many of the other towns along the valleys of mountain streams, escaped very serious results of the high water caused by the general downpour of rain that lasted almost without pause for 60 hours.

Wm. Mather says he never saw the Bow rise as fast. Mr. Sanson reported one and one half inches of a fall of rain for hours.

The bridge crossing Stony Creek is no more, and a smaller one at Canmore is also gone. Repairs on same have started at once.

Whiskey Creek, where it crossed under the track just east of the station changed its course, going down the excursion spur, running under the station, completely filling the station basement and then coming out at the west end of the building, flooding the road to the water tank with a foot or more water eventually getting into Forty Mile Creek.

The Bow Bridge had a narrow escape and another 24 hours of rain would no doubt have carried this old timer to the Bow Falls.

One thing everyone agreed on, the rain stopped only just in time.

Several washouts occurred on the auto road between the Gap and Canmore and other places on Tunnel Mountain Drive, Muskrat and Marten Streets and up to Sundance Canyon. Most of these were early taken care of and the vehicle traffic was not in any extent interrupted.

July 5th - Fine forenoon, rain afternoon
To Healy Creek with John McKay, Holland and Tex Wood to show them work on trail, left them and pack outfit near Healy Crossing to build culvert over muskeg, brought horses to town, 12 miles rode.

July 6th - Fine, showery forenoon and evening
To Castle Mountain Detention Camp with speeder and letter for Capt. Spencer from Supt. Clarke, left hand speeder at Massive, motor broke on way home, got section man to bring me to Sawback, took Phillips' hand speeder and came to Banff, arrived home 8:30, 40 miles by track on speeder.

July 7th - Fine, some showers

To Healy and Brewster Creeks, took horses to Wood's camp, measured trail cut by Ballard from Healy Creek Trail to Brewster Creek - 2 ¼ miles, 18 miles rode and walked.

July 8th - Fine, cloudy

Got order from Supt. Clarke to get out with Ford car, demonstration with fire auto - to get moving pictures for advertising purposes, stringing out wet hose in afternoon and fixed up more pack saddles.

July 13th - Cloudy

To Forty Mile Creek via Mount Edith Pass with J. Warren, getting camp outfit of Tex Wood out of water, got 1 tent, 2 pack bags and 3 blankets, blankets and tent badly torn by rocks, 10 miles rode and walked.

July 14th - Rain forenoon and afternoon

Up to office forenoon, to Hot Springs in evening, Mr. Stewart notified me that a big black bear was bothering the Hot Springs people, rode up in evening accompanied by J. Warren, ran into Mr. Bear near Alpine Club, put bullet through him at shoulder, laid as if dead for several minutes but finally got away, found lots of blood and strips of meat where bullet had blown his shoulder out, had to quit tracking him as it got dark, was notified by Stewart that 2 bears were troubling.

July 15th - Rain

Left stables at daylight with J. Warren, up to Alpine Club and looked through bush but could not locate bear, blood on bushes for short distance, feel certain bear must have bled to death, went on to Hot Springs - wet through, got dried out at Government Bath House and waited all afternoon for second black bear. Ashton came down from Villa and told us that the bear had just left which was a lie as he does not seem to want bears killed. Went up to Grand View Villa for dinner, Mr. Sibbald came to Villa while we were walking down to Garbage Grounds - bear came to Villa, Mr. Sibbald fired one shot at him but 4 of us today were unable to locate this bear, feel if hit in chest where Chief aimed for would surely die, the bush being thick around this spot one does not often get a second shot, so that an animal can get so far away even if badly hit as a bear will carry away a lot of lead, 10 miles rode and walked.

July 16th - Showery

Up to office forenoon, to Hot Springs afternoon, Miss McCall phoned down to say that bear was at garbage barrel at rear of hotel, went to hotel with W.W. Cory's two sons and J. Warren, we waited till dark but Mr. Bear did not show up, 5 or 6 miles rode.

July 17th - Rain

To Hot Springs, waiting for bear all day, no sign of him until just after dark, was up at Grand Villa when bear appeared below at Hot Springs, J. Warren shot it through the shoulder but could not get second shot as the bear rolled down the hill when hit roaring wildly, too dark to hunt bush.

July 18th - Cloudy, showers

Went to Hot Springs trying to locate bear but no luck, went to Buffalo Park with Mr. Sibbald and vet to doctor young bull, 9 or 10 miles rode.

July 20th - Fine, warm

Out to Buffalo Park to skin out buffalo head in forenoon, left skull on rock for flies to clean, to race track in afternoon, 10 miles rode.

July 21st - Clear, warm

Took buffalo head to taxidermist to see if possible to mount but he said it was no good, to Upper Hot Springs and Spray Valley in afternoon, 10 miles rode.

July 23rd - Clear and warm

Helped Tex Wood and Howard Sibbald pack up, went up Basin Road and Loop in afternoon, 10 miles rode, to Hot Springs after supper looking for large black bear till 10 p.m.

July 24th - Warm, thunder during night

Fixing fence in horse pasture forenoon, to Buffalo Park for saddle horse in afternoon, to Hot Springs in evening - looking for bear, sealed Remington 22 cal. rifle for A. Carlson, 12 miles rode.

July 25th - Fine forenoon, cloudy afternoon

Banff to Mystic Lake with J. Warren, Lou Cory and Wilf Cory via Mount Edith Pass, 15 miles rode, camped on Forty Mile Creek at mouth of Mystic Creek and walked up to Mystic, had good luck fishing.

July 28th - Cloudy, some rain

Mystic to Sawback Lake over Sawback Summit, 15 or 16 miles rode, no luck in Sawback Lake, fishing in creek good.

July 29th - Showery

Sawback Lake to Windy Cabin on Panther River and Wigmore Creek by way of Carthew Summit, 25 miles rode and walked, noticed Wigmore and Carthew Creeks had been about 3 or 4 feet above usual height at time of floods.

July 30th - Fine forenoon, thunderstorm afternoon

To Harrison Lake and return, fished half day, we had good luck fishing, 8 or 9 miles rode.

July 31st - Fine forenoon, rain afternoon

Windy Cabin (on Panther) to Banff, stopped at Stony Creek for lunch, 25 miles rode.

August 1915

August 3rd - Showery

Motor Road, Loop and Spray Valley, loaded auto for Massive, 10 miles rode, went to lube station, set traps for a Mr. Rat.

August 4th - Fine

Packed remainder of material for Red Earth Cabin and loaded auto for Massive, to station forenoon, 9 or 10 miles walked and rode, caught Mr. Rat last night.

August 9th - Warm

To pasture forenoon, caught two mares belonging to Boyce and returned them to him, east on Tote Road to Forty Mile Creek, at Buffalo Park, 10 miles rode.

August 14th - Fine and warm

Packing wire to Sulphur Mountain, caught horses with Sibbald, packed up W.W. Cory's outfit, 15 miles rode.

August 16th - Showery, lots of thunder
Patrolling Motor Road and tracks keeping lookout for escaped aliens from Detention Camp, sealed guns, 10 miles rode and walked.

August 17th - Showery, thunder
On lookout for aliens on Motor Road and tracks, sealed guns for Cuthbert, 7 or 8 miles rode and walked.

August 19th - Showery
To Healy Creek for pack left by Mr. Cory and party and to pasture on return, 14 miles rode.

August 21st - Fine
Up Motor Road to Boyce camp and 5 mile board and to Loop in afternoon, put out hose to dry, 17 or 18 miles rode.

August 26th - Fine
To Bankhead forenoon with Graham and handed him over to Scotty Wright, up Spray Valley in afternoon, 15 miles rode.

August 27th - Fine
Up town and sealed rifles for packer going out with Brewster, out with auto taking first lesson driving with McAulay, west on Auto Road, put out fire hose, 16 miles walked and auto.

August 29th - Fine
Up to CPR stables to seal rifles for Hodges and party.

September 1915
September 1st - Cloudy, warm
Up town, rolled up fire hose, around to sawmill, shot coyote near section man's house (old dog), saw Mumford pulling out, down looking for young moose in afternoon, met Phillips and wife near the station leaving town, 8 or 9 miles walked, sealed rifle - 22 auto Winchester belonging to Scott Ashley.

September 3rd - Fine
Sundance Canyon and Spray, Hot Springs in afternoon and back to Hot Springs at 10 p.m. with Tex Wood and shot big black bear at 1:15 a.m., found him at daylight (weight about

350), turned horses out to pasture, 10 miles rode and drove, sealed guns for Fred Hussey.

September 5th - Warm

About south end of town after coyote, up to stables and storeroom, helped Curren and Wood away for south country, walked to Buffalo Park, 5 or 6 miles walked.

September 9th - Fair, cold

Getting outfit ready for HES, out to Buffalo Park in afternoon, in charge as Woodworth got attacked by old bull yak, 10 miles rode.

The Banff Crag & Canyon - September 11th, 1915

Tossed by bull yak at Buffalo Park

Well-known Banff citizen narrowly escapes death when yak charges

Ben Woodworth narrowly escaped death last Thursday. While doing his rounds in the yak enclosure the old bull took a run at him and before he could escape was knocked down and then picked up by the ferocious animal's horns and tossed over his back. He managed to escape to a place of safety near the fence, and from there he was assisted to the house. An examination proved a serious contusion of the hip, back, chest and two fractures in the shoulder, a broken thumb as well as a severe nerve shock to his system. Last report before going to press from the hospital is that he is as well as can be expected.

September 10th - Cloudy, cold

Out at Buffalo Park all day tending to duties of caretaker.

September 13th - Cloudy

To Healy Creek Cabin, brought Cuthbert's party to town, released horses in afternoon, 16 miles rode.

September 14th - Cloudy, warmer

To Healy Cabin, met Tex and Curren, came to town, put Brewster horses in pasture, 15 or 16 miles rode.

September 16th - Fine

Police court morning and afternoon, outfit fined $25.00 and costs for illegal possession of elk hide.

The Banff Crag & Canyon - September 18th, 1915
Sensation Caused in Police Court
Possession of elk hide responsible for another charge

In connection with Police Court proceedings this week which have caused so much interest around town, the fine had hardly been paid, and Frank Eaton given notice of appeal, when somewhat of a sensation was caused among the audience by Corporal Baker of the RNWMP serving each of the accused in the previous case with notice to defend, they having been found in possession of a wapiti or elk hide, contrary to Sections 61 and 69 of the Park Regulations.

This case followed the goat head on the afternoon of last Thursday with Frank Eaton defending and C. Adams acting for the Government.

The first witness called was Chas. V. Phillips, who stated that he was sent by the chief game warden of the park, with Walter Peyto to arrest the above-mentioned accused and found them near Healy Creek, about nine or ten miles from the water shed of the Rockies, which designates the boundary between Alberta and B.C. The party was escorted into Banff and the entire outfit taken over by the Park authorities. Walter Peyto and Howard Sibbald being cross-examined, it appeared that an elk hide had been discovered among the accused's effects and Howard Sibbald swore that the elk hide was possibly three to four weeks old. Walter Avery, game warden of Golden, B.C. stated he came here in the interests of his province in the capacity that he held, and had examined the elk hide, and in his opinion it was less than three weeks old. Stipendiary Magistrate Carpenter found the party guilty of having in their possession a "green elk hide" contrary to the laws of the Canadian National Parks, fining them $25.00 each without costs.

September 17th to 30th
Buffalo Park all day.

October 1915
October 1st to October 8th
Working at Buffalo Park in Woodworth's place, shot two coyotes on 8th.

October 9th to 14th

Sick with tonsillitis.

October 15th

Helped Bevan and Wood out to Bankhead with horses.

October 21st

Home, wife sick, took walk to station at night.

October 22nd

At police court listening to trial of Crosby and Jordan for shooting in the park, magistrate's decision, $50.00 and costs and confiscated pack trains.

The Banff Crag & Canyon - October 23rd, 1915

Lou Crosby Would A Shootin' Go

First Time Park Regulations as to confiscation of entire pack train enforced - outfit valued at $1,000.00

Magistrate Carpenter's court was crowded yesterday at the trial of L. S. Crosby, general manager of the Brewster Transport and Trading companies, and Art Jordan, barn boss for the Transport Co., on a charge of killing sheep within the limits of the park. Charles Adams appeared for the prosecution, Frank Eaton for the accused.

Crosby and Jordan entered pleas of not guilty.

Game Guardians Wright and Bevan testified to finding the remains of a dead sheep about two miles inside the park boundary, off the Red Deer or Cascade Trail, October 7th, followed by the tracks of the horses to a camp occupied by the accused, where they found the heads of two sheep. Wright picked up an empty cartridge shell near the dead sheep, an 8 - 12 mm, which corresponded with the calibre of Crosby's rifle.

Wright also stated that in conversation with Crosby the latter asserted that the sheep had been shot outside the boundary of the Park and had run to where the carcass was found (some two miles) before falling.

Howard Sibbald and Tex Wood corroborated the evidence given by the previous witnesses, based on a visit to the scene of the shooting, October 12th. Both gave a very interocting and oloar account of the passage of the bullet through the sheep which caused beyond doubt, instant death. The spine was shattered for several inches between the head and shoulders.

Court adjourned until 8 o'clock when it was found the

defendants, Crosby and Jordan were guilty as charged and they were fined $50.00 each and the entire pack train of ten horses and camp equipage including three guns confiscated. The outfit was worth $1,000.00.

Another case on a similar charge is pending against Crosby and Jordan.

November 1915
November 3rd
Changed horses from moose pasture to lower buffalo pasture in forenoon, fixed up storehouse in afternoon and looked for coyotes down around Moffatt's Ranch.

November 8th - Cold
Went to big meadow west of Banff with Wood after horses, branded same in afternoon and took them to lower buffalo pasture, 12 miles rode.

November 10th - Clear and cold
Walked along track to depot and to stable, helped Warren and Wood round up horses and travelled as far as Bankhead Station with them.

November 12th - Cold
Upper Anthracite Road, Spray Avenue removing Crosby's outfit, shot female coyote, saw one with mange, 8 or 9 miles rode.

November 14th - Clear and cold
Left Banff with 2 teams and harness to go to Field Intern Camp, went as far as Castle, had lunch with Phillips and stayed all night with Fyfe, paid $1.50 for 2 bales of hay, 19 miles rode.

November 15th - Clear and cold, snow towards evening
Castle to Lake Louise, about 14 or 15 inches of snow, west of Eldon saw several coyotes, shot 1 at mileage 113, rode about 19 miles.

November 18th - Cloudy
Lower Buffalo Park, catching Persian ram and shipping same to Yorkton, Saskatchewan in forenoon, to Buffalo Park moving horses from sheep pasture to moose pasture out at night after coyotes, 8 miles rode and drove.

November 19th - Clear, cold

Along back of Cave and Basin with gang of aliens cutting line for telephone all day.

November 24th - Mild

About town forenoon, Motor Road, Squaw Mountain, shot 1 coyote, found yearling deer's carcass apparently killed by coyotes, used for coyote bait.

November 29th

To Healy Cabin by way of Sundance with Mumford, hauled three bales of wire along trail and left Phillips to finish line to cabin, 12 miles walked and drove.

December 1915

December 1st - Cold, west wind

To Massive, stopped at Sawback and working on telephone line till night, stayed at Massive overnight, 12 miles by speeder.

December 6th - Mild

To Hot Springs in forenoon, to Healy Creek to where Fyfe and Curren were working on telephone line to get more wire, 12 miles rode.

December 8th - Snow forenoon, rain afternoon

Up to office forenoon, shot stray collie dog forenoon, down to pasture looking up horses in afternoon, walked 4 or 5 miles.

December 10th - Clear forenoon, cloudy afternoon

Started for Massive with HES car, met Phillips, returned to Banff along track to Banff Station in evening, 5 or 6 miles walked.

December 16th - Clear, mild

Working on telephone line all day, finished line to Massive Cabin, came to Banff with HES, walked and pushed motor speeder 11 miles, some trip.

December 18th - Clear, mild

To Healy Creek Cabin with Fyfe and Curren, helped finish telephone line from Banff to Healy Creek, helped H.E. Sibbald connect wire at his house, 12 miles rode.

December 20th - Fine, west wind
About town forenoon, drove Frenchy's horses, 8 miles walked and drove.

December 30th - Cold, north east wind, some snow
In forenoon up town and by Forty Mile and river, west across Lakes to big meadow, across river to back of alien camp following telephone line, 5 or 6 miles walked.

Government Bath House at Upper Hot Springs - 1915. Whyte Museum of the Canadian Rockies. V573 NA66-447.

East Gate - Rocky Mountains Park. Whyte Museum of the Canadian Rockies. V263 NA71-3436.

Alpine Club Building. Whyte Museum of the Canadian Rockies. V263 NA71-17.

Drs. Brett and Atkin (standing) with Mrs. Brett's dog Victor, in front of Sanitarium 1912-13. Whyte Museum of the Canadian Rockies. V484 NA29-401.

Nineteen Sixteen

January 1916

January 3rd - Zero all day, snow all day

Motor Road, Vermilion Lakes, along through hills east of Tunnel, along south side of Tunnel back to town, saw several coyotes on river, too far away for shooting, 5 or 6 miles walked.

January 5th - Cold west wind, clear

Down around bush near station and Forty Mile Creek, up to office helping Sibbald fix motor, looking up Steve Hope for dog license, 4 or 5 miles walked.

January 6th - Cold, west wind

Motor Road, station, helping at office, fetched Wood to station with HES in forenoon, got J. Simpson to shoot coyote having gone up town without rifle in forenoon, helped Sibbald fix batteries for speeder, walked up track with Wood to Second Lake, crossed First Lake to Motor Road and back to town, 8 miles walked.

January 7th - Cold, west wind

Around coyote traps near station, up town, west across meadows west of town to river again, down river to town in forenoon, around Loop and Bankhead Road and down to Bow River at mouth of Forty Mile Creek with Wood, 12 miles walked and rode.

January 8th - Cold forenoon, mild afternoon

Up Bow River and across lakes to Motor Road, Healy Creek and along telephone line, found 3 insulators broken off trees, wire not touching ground, shot 1 coyote, 10 miles walked and rode.

January 12th - 38 below, very cold, warmer afternoon

About town, went to station for Sibbald for parcel, looking around station in afternoon and evening, looking for coyotes in moonlight, 2 or 3 miles walked.

January 13th - 32 below, west wind

Down across Bow River to Garbage Grounds with Wood to get traps in forenoon, down around river where Brewsters are cutting ice - trying to get shot at coyote, unable to shoot as every time I came on to him he was directly between house and me or in line with street, out again in moonlight after supper, 5 or 6 miles walked.

The Banff Crag & Canyon - January 15th, 1916
Cold Wave Hits Banff

The cold wave which has been creeping over the northwest did not pass up Banff. It started with the New Year, Monday night, January 3rd, the mercury dropping to 22 below and the following night it fell still lower reaching the 25 mark.

Then followed a brief breathing spell of mountain weather until Monday, Jan. 10th, when the mercury tried to kick the bottom out of the glass and made a record of 46 degrees below zero. During the following four days there was little let up to the steady cold, the thermometer ranging from 20 to 40 below day and night.

This is the coldest weather experienced in Banff for many years. Eight years ago for a week, the mercury hung among the 40's and many old timers had cause to remember it. Wednesday, Feb. 4th, 1914, the government instrument registered 41 below, but the cold snap lasted only for a day.

January 17th - Cold forenoon, milder afternoon
Up to office and down along Forty Mile Creek, along Motor Road, up Squaw Mountain to Tote Road, east on Tote Road and fixing traps, saw cook from wood camp pulling sleigh with damage coming into Banff Station, he had large brown dog, turned horses in yard for exercise, 5 miles walked.
January 19th - Mild
Down around Bow River and station looking for coyotes, along hills east of Tunnel Mountain, out after supper to station, shot one male coyote on track at west yard limit, went up and got poison from Jim Simpson, 6 miles walked.
January 20th - Mild
Up track to western yard limit, Loop and Hot Springs, shot one female coyote on river opposite yard limit, very mangy, hide no good, out after supper to water tank, shot one male

coyote with shotgun, found he had mange too, 12 miles rode and walked, disease nature's way of thinning them out like the rabbits.

January 21st - Cold, N.E. wind, snow all day

Caught young dog coyote in trap, he was also very bad with mange, hide no good, no money in supplying own ammunition at that, 3 miles walked.

January 23rd - Snow all day, worse that yesterday, very cold, about 25 below, strong wind

To Post Office for mail, at home rest of day, the most snow I have seen in Banff for years, all baits and traps will be buried and any coyotes that had picked up baits before storm, expect coyotes will be very apt to kill after this big storm.

January 24th - Clear but very cold, about 2 feet of snow fell

Went down along track to station, and dug traps out of snow, no animal life stirring at all, up town for mail.

January 27th - Clear and cold all day, sun dog in afternoon

Down around station and up to Post Office and government office, helped cut down dead tree up river of Museum, 4 miles walked.

January 29th - Clear and cold forenoon, clear warmer afternoon till evening, very cold, glass dropped very quickly

Up town and to office forenoon, along Motor Road to 2 mile board and across First Lake to tracks and home, 7 miles walked and snowshoed, saw very large coyote at about 300 yards eating at deer just killed, he got away before I had a chance to shoot, deer was a last spring fawn and had just been killed as carcass was hot, had been caught up on rocks and fought its way down to creek bottom and Motor Road, had poison with me, put some in meat and put up notice on road, had been ham strung and torn up very bad, heard several coyotes yapping up on hill, other deer were feeding among big firs.

The Banff Crag & Canyon - January 29th, 1916
Banff in Storm King's Grip

Sunday's Storm most severe in Twenty Years - Reminiscences of 1896

For the past several days Banff has been in the grip of the storm king and although there has been no actual suffering, many people have been greatly inconvenienced by frozen water pipes and zero weather in their homes.

Snow started to fall last Friday afternoon and continued without intermission until Sunday afternoon when it culminated in a miniature blizzard. Some 26 inches of snow fell on the level, and the gale of Sunday piled the snow in drifts rendering navigation of the streets almost impossible. The mercury dropped rapidly, reaching the extreme low point of 46.5 below zero during Sunday night.

All trains from the west were cancelled owing to trouble in the mountains. The first eastbound train to arrive in Banff for a period of 48 hours reached here Tuesday afternoon and it was made up at Revelstoke.

The extreme cold, ranging from 30 to 40 below zero, in addition to the cutting wind kept citizens confined to their homes, no one venturing to leave the shelter of their fireside unless absolutely compelled to do so.

This was the most severe storm experienced in Banff in twenty years.

February 1916

February 3rd - Cold forenoon, mild afternoon
Motor Road, Lakes, Anthracite, 14 miles walked and drove, with Morrison to Duncan's at Anthracite, saw lots of lynx tracks.

February 8th - Cold, N.E. wind
West on track to mileage 83, across river to Canyon Road, Motor Road to 6 mile in afternoon with H.E. Sibbald, met Phillips, set trap for coyote at rear of animal meat house, out after night putting out bait for coyotes, 17 miles drove and snowshoed, noticed deer at sand hill not eating hay, cleaned up at sulphur spring.

February 14th - Mild, soft underfoot
Along moose fence to Tote Road, west to Motor Road, up town, Hot Springs in afternoon, got one coyote with bait at Hot Springs but others had eaten him almost all up, 7 or 8 miles walked and rode.

February 20th - Mild

Falls and Motor Road, 5 or 6 miles rode, found car shed unlocked and H.E. Sibbald's gun gone, perhaps Phillips has it.

February 23rd - Cloudy, mild

Motor Road, Spray Valley, on Squaw Mountain, west on track, back along river, have not seen coyote tracks for some time although sometimes hear them howl at night, 10 miles rode and walked.

March 1916

March 12th - Snow all night, little sun after noon

Called out at five o' clock to fire next door, stayed with fire throwing water on while B. Fay went for fire brigade, got fire under control by time fire brigade reached house, should be alarms at ends of some of the streets.

March 16th - Fine

West on track to end of meadows, skinned out head of South African sheep and salted scalp and put skull in with eagles, beast had broken its neck, working on fire car remainder of afternoon, 8 miles walked.

March 20th - Fine

Heard and saw 2 robins at 7 a.m. this morning near house, Loop and Spray Valley, Motor Road to foot of Squaw Mountain, 12 miles rode and walked.

March 22nd - Fine, snow during night

Along moose pasture to Tote Road, west to Motor Road, along Bankhead Road, 8 miles walked, heard 5 aliens had escaped.

March 23rd - Fine

Along Sundance Road, falls and Spray in forenoon, Buffalo Park and dam in afternoon, 12 miles rode and walked, hurt thumb on right hand in forenoon, bruised joint, very sore, doctor bandaged, told me to rest it.

March 25th - Fine

Along track and through bush east of Moffatt's, along lower road to Anthracite, went up to Johnson Lake or Blue Lake with Vick and Rodd, came onto a man living in shack in thick pines, told me he had been here eight years, no one has seen him at any time, he talked good English, intend to investigate him again, 20 miles rode and walked.

March 28th - Fine

Working on speeder with Wood, rigged it up as hand speeder as engine is no good, went to shack at Anthracite with Morrison, P.C. Walker and Deputy Warden Wright, did not find man at home, Wright and Police Constable searched but found nothing suspicious, Mr. Morrison and I saw four deer near shack and noticed they were not at all scared, 12 miles rode.

April 1916

April 1st - 5 inches of snow on ground forenoon, some snow during day

Government yard grinding axes with Tex Wood all day, 4 miles walked.

April 4th - Snow

Banff to Healy Creek Cabin repairing telephone line (with Wood), could not find break in wire, 14 miles rode and walked.

April 5th - Fine

Banff to Healy Creek Cabin repairing line, met Phillips who had found break in wire between Healy Creek and Bow River, 14 miles rode and walked.

April 8th - Fine

Banff to Healy Creek with Wood, worked all day taking large rocks out of ford in Healy Creek at upper crossing on Boyce trail, 12 miles rode, found doctor and nurse in house when I reached home, daughter born 6:30.

April 9th - Cloudy forenoon, rain afternoon, some snow evening - 7:30

Heard from section boss a female (old) deer lying in ice on CPR right of way 1 mile east of Banff, went down track and saw deer - carcass had been there a long time, it had a broken neck from hitting the wire fence of moose pasture

51

apparently having been scared by passing train, 4 miles walked.

April 15th - Fine

Out in forenoon with Sanson after specimens of duck and crows, Motor Road and Buffalo Park, 12 miles walked and rode.

April 17th - Fine, heavy snow at night

Working on fire car all day with H.E. Sibbald and Bevan, started for Canmore but blew a tire at Buffalo Park, came back to stable.

April 19th - Fine

Put new tube in rear wheel of auto truck in forenoon, west on Auto Road to Sawback with Lorne Orr in his auto trying to locate eagle.

April 25th - Fine, warm

Working on telephone extension in forenoon, went to Canmore in afternoon with HES in fire auto, got stuck in bad part of road at Anthracite, 30 miles by auto.

April 26th - Fine

Cut posts up Cave Avenue for aliens to peel, posts to be used on arch at eastern entrance to park, along Spray Avenue, down through bush south of CPR Hotel, to falls and Loop in afternoon, 12 miles walked and rode.

May 1916

May 1st - Fine, rain at night

Washed auto forenoon and went with Sanson getting specimens of duck along Bow, got some he had not seen before, Hot Springs in afternoon, 8 miles walked and rode.

May 2nd - Fine, very warm

Along Motor Road, up to stores - overhauling fire hose, up Spray Valley in afternoon to new bridge, one foreman with aliens had small fire get away, guards would not let aliens help him put it out, 12 miles walked and rode.

May 3rd - Fine

Cave Avenue and Recreation Grounds, and along Bow River, working on telephone at Chief's house forenoon, putting coal oil in stagnant water to kill mosquitoes in afternoon, 8 miles walked and rode.

May 4th - Fine

Along Cave Avenue and to Recreation Grounds, putting oil on stagnant water and getting man from McAulay to dig ditches, down Canmore Trail twice, 35 miles rode and auto.

May 5th - Some rain

Burning brush on Cave Avenue and cleaning out ditches to let water off along edge of meadows in forenoon, east on Canmore Trail with Shancross in big motor truck to bring back driving gear of fire auto, 18 miles rode and motored.

May 6th - Rain

Working all afternoon at Deegan's garage putting in new axles of Ford fire truck, took same to car on Canmore Road and fixed up car with HES and Deegan, 15 miles by motor.

May 7th - Fine

Along Motor Road by sawmill, Chinaman's garden and Moffatt's, saw black and brown bears outside Chinaman's fence, 6 or 7 miles walked.

May 11th - Cloudy, cool

Putting out coal oil for mosquitoes, went to Bankhead Station, searched elk pasture for lynx said to be in there, down around Moffatt's in evening, 12 miles rode and walked.

May 12th - Fine, cool

Falls and hatchery, putting out coal oil, up to sucker hole and Sawback, helped Vick get suckers for bear, got horse's shoes removed in afternoon, 20 miles rode.

May 15th - Fine, cool

Cave Avenue, Hot Springs, 10 miles rode, helped Jordan and Wood get logs for arch at Kananaskis and peeled and loaded same, put out coal oil.

May 17th - Fine, rain shower at noon

West on Motor Road to Sawback Hill, Loop and Sundance Road with HES and Super, 20 miles by auto, put out coal oil for mosquitoes.

May 22nd - Cloudy, some snow

Banff to Healy Creek Cabin repairing telephone wire, met

Wood at cabin, saw fresh tracks of bear near cabin and along gravel bars near Healy Creek, 16 miles rode and walked.

May 23rd - Rain and snow

West along track to station, through to Moffatt's and Chinaman's yards, came onto grizzly bear suddenly while following Forty Mile Creek about 200 yards from station and about 150 yards from Moffatt's house, stayed around most of day and went out after supper, stayed till dark, 5 or 6 miles walked.

May 24th - Snow all day, 6 inches on ground by morning

Walked through by Moffatt's in forenoon, saw nothing of bear, built small platform in trees near bait with J. Warren - afternoon, came down about 7:30 with Warren, got up on platform and waited, bear appeared about 15 minutes later but did not come to bait for another 15 or 20 minutes, when he did we put two bullets into him (one of which entered his lungs and the other lodged in his heart), after which he ran 75 yards and crossed the creek and climbed bank on other side, left carcass lying up at Moffatt's overnight, 5 miles walked.

May 25th - Cloudy

Went down to Moffatt's and skinned bear in forenoon after going up town to see HES, skinned out bear and feet in afternoon, and partly fleshed hide, not very large for grizzly, 4 miles walked.

The Banff Crag & Canyon - May 27th, 1916
Shoot Bad Bear

For several nights a Chinese gardener, who lives near the old Brett mill site across Forty Mile Creek ... and his garden had been culled of choice morsels of green goods by a hungry bear. The game wardens had been instructed to keep a watchful eye for the marauder - as once a bear becomes addicted to pilfering food from gardens and houses the brute becomes a menace to citizens and is marked as an outlaw, whose sentence is death.

Wednesday night Game Wardens Peyto and Warren discovered the bear prowling about in the rear of Moffatt's ice house. They took no chances, both firing at once and both bullets found billets. An autopsy revealed a chunk of lead embedded in the heart, yet despite this he ran 50 yards and swam the creek before giving up the ghost.

Bruin was a grizzly, about the size of the silver-tips in the zoological gardens and some 4 years old.

May 30th - Rain all day

Got horse ready to go to Canmore to meet Bevan with horses, but telephone line - long distance broken - could not get him on phone, rode 5 miles about town.

June 1916

June 2nd - Fine

Travelled through yak pasture looking for a coyote, found young yak partly eaten and old cow yak stuck in mud in creek with calf, phoned town to have Woodworth sent down, got Melville to help me pull cow out of water, after which I took calf from cow and gave cow a drink of hot water and ginger, did not see Woodworth till after I had been home and had dinner, saw cow in afternoon and she seemed lots better, took some horses to lower pasture and caught up Super's horse and other cayuse, 10 miles rode.

June 3rd - Cloudy forenoon, warm afternoon

Took mare and cayuse to shop to get shoes on for Bevan to take north, gave Bevan outfit from storeroom and went to Buffalo Park with him after noon and helped him catch his horses and also bought up three to the stable, 12 miles walked and rode.

June 10th - Fine

Buffalo Park, caught Mumford's horses, took same to blacksmith shop, west along Motor Road to Sawback hill, train men reported some animal killing Moffatt's calves, I went up with Moffatt, saw big coyote on edge of lake, I took a shot at him and hit him (about 250 yards), never heard coyote howl like he did, he just rolled in the mud and howled like a dog.

June 13th - Cloudy
Loop and Garbage Ground with aliens, cleaning up and burning, 6 miles walked.

June 15th - Fine, hot
Had gang of aliens cutting new trail from Cave Avenue to Hot Springs Road, finished up trail at 5:45, 5 miles walked.

June 16th
Took four horses to pasture at lower buffalo field, turned out, caught up three more, had shoes removed off sorrel and black and turned them out in upper pasture, saw bay horse had been bleeding from nose, very weak, 10 miles rode.

June 17th
Got bay saddle horse shod in forenoon, gave Capt. Burrough black horse of Brewster bunch, rode along Cave Avenue and through new trail to Hot Springs Road, mixed paint for arch at Kananaskis, 12 miles rode and walked.

June 19th - Rain, heavy in afternoon
To lower buffalo pasture to inspect horse that had died, cause of death apparently broken blood vessel from kick in head, up to office and got Sanson to explain how to fix barometers, rounded up two saddle horses in afternoon, 10 miles rode and walked.

June 20th - Rain all day
To lower buffalo pasture with Curren for horses, brought up Wright's packhorse, grinding axes in afternoon with Wood, upper horse pasture almost under water.

June 21st - Warm, cloudy
Up Spray Valley to see bridge at Eau Claire camp, found approach to bridge washed out, but it can be swung around when water goes down, prospecting for new trail from Spray Bridge to old pack trail on Rundle Mountain, 20 miles rode and walked.

June 22nd - Fine, warm
To lower pasture forenoon with Wood to get saddle horse, to lower pasture in afternoon to get pack horse to take camp to Forty Mile Creek, got packs made up ready to hit the trail in the morning early, 15 miles rode and walked.

June 23rd - Warm, rain shower afternoon

Banff to Forty Mile Creek via Mount Edith Pass and working on new bridge over creek till 9:30, no feed for horses, only oats, bad drift at top at pass, 12 miles walked and rode, shot female coyote near hill on Motor Road.

June 27th - Fine

Working on bridge all day till 10 p.m.

June 30th - Warm

Went along Rundle Trail south some distance with Warren, helped him pack, caught Wood's saddle horse and helped him fix up rig to use at Healy Creek, went along Canyon Road and caught his pack horse in afternoon, took fishing line away from kids, 12 miles rode and walked.

July 1916

July 1st - Fine

Falls and Spray Valley, Buffalo Park, Motor Road and Forty Mile and Whiskey Creeks, 12 miles walked and rode, took up several lines left in creek overnight by kids.

July 2nd - Showery

Buffalo Park and elk pasture with Woodworth, found cow elk dead with both hind legs broke up about 1 foot above hock, apparently having jumped snow fence, being heavy in calf and possibly caught herself up, about town and creeks in evening, 10 miles walked and rode.

July 5th - Fine

To buffalo pasture to get horses for Caine to take to Laggan, repairing fire auto - changed tire and put new rubber hose connection on radiator, mending telephone west of Cave and Basin, 12 miles rode and walked.

July 6th - Fine, hot

To Buffalo Park and Healy Cabin, 16 miles rode and walked, helped Walcott move pack outfit - 8 packs, and took them to Healy Cabin.

July 11th - Fine

Buffalo Park all day, caught up horses from pasture, brought to town, also brought Woodworth's mare to town and got her shod, 12 miles rode, walked to Buffalo Park - evening.

July 12th - Fine showers at night

Fixed telephone line across Bow Bridge, along Cave Avenue and short cut to Hot Springs Road, to falls and CPR Hotel, Tunnel Mountain Drive and Buffalo Park with Norwegian Forestry Man (Anton Smith), 15 or 16 miles rode.

July 13th - Fine, rain storm at night

About town forenoon, up at garage helping old man fix fire auto, lent Indian torn teepees.

July 16th - Very hot, Sunday

Banff to Kananaskis arch and back to Banff with HES and Phillips, met Tom Staple at arch, had lots of trouble with tire, 56 miles motored.

July 17th - Fine, hot

Went to station and office, checked Sibbald's luggage, saw Duke leave Banff [Editor's note - Duke of Connaught], fixed tire on fire auto, took car to garage, 5 miles walked.

July 20th - Fine

To Buffalo Pasture for horses and helping Warren get pack outfit ready for Mr. Cory's party, 8 miles walked and rode.

July 22nd - Cloudy, rain all forenoon and night, fine afternoon

Fixed up fire pump forenoon, up to office and sent away weekly fire report to Chief Warden, met Warren at 9:30 p.m. and helped him with packs and horses.

July 24th - Cloudy, rain evening

Took horses to pasture and went up to yard and office, got orders to get to Hot Springs, to Hot Springs in afternoon to see about some campers, reported that no place fit for camping at Hot Springs, danger of fire too great, 12 miles rode and walked.

July 30th - Hot

About town all day, gave Curren a horse to go and hunt his saddle horse.

August 1916

August 2ⁿᵈ - Cloudy

Up to government yard forenoon, put tracks together and hose on wheels, packing pump and fitting for Caine, Cave Avenue and falls, large crowd in town, 10 miles rode.

August 3ʳᵈ - Rain

Shipped fire pump to Caine forenoon, mended hand speeder in afternoon, 5 or 6 miles rode, got horse shod.

August 4ᵗʰ - Hot

Banff to Castle Mountain and return, fixing telephone wire on Fyfe's division with Phillips and H.E. Sibbald, 36 miles by motor speeder.

August 10ᵗʰ

About town and to office, Spray Valley to old Eau Claire Bridge to see if possible to fix up, 20 miles walked and rode.

August 15ᵗʰ - Fine

To Observatory with Furnell's man to fix phone and wire leading from Hot Springs to mountain, 14 miles rode and walked.

August 16ᵗʰ - Showery

About town forenoon, out to Minnewanka with Phillips to overhaul fire pump for Wright, 20 miles walked and motored.

August 18ᵗʰ - Fine

To Hot Springs to see what damage bear had done, found one window broken.

August 19ᵗʰ - Showery

To pasture for horses to take out J.B. Harkin, helped Sibbald get outfit ready, 10 miles rode and walked.

August 23ʳᵈ - Fine

Took Sanson's camp to end of Cascade Summit Trail via Squaw Mountain, 12 miles rode and walked.

August 30ᵗʰ - Fine forenoon, cloudy afternoon

Banff to Canmore Cabin and return, and west to Healy Cabin, 45 miles by auto, took building material to each place.

August 31ˢᵗ - Fine
Motor Road, Loop and Spray Valley, painted gasoline cans in forenoon, 12 miles rode, sealed rifle for Mr. Brady - Winchester.

September 1916
September 1ˢᵗ - Fine forenoon, cloudy afternoon
West on Motor Road to 7 mile board twice with supplies for Wood, out to Buffalo Park in afternoon, helped put moose in pasture, also shot sick yearling mountain sheep, 32 miles rode and motored.
September 6ᵗʰ - Fine
To end of Cascade Summit Trail and brought in Sanson's camp outfit and fossils, 12 or 13 miles rode, saw HES at night and got orders to go with Wood.
September 7ᵗʰ - Fine
To ford of Simpson River with Wood via Healy Creek on our way to Kootenay Valley for horses lost by HES and J.B. Harkin, 25 miles rode.
September 8ᵗʰ - Rain
Simpson to Vermilion, 15 or 16 miles rode.
September 9ᵗʰ - Rain
Vermilion to Kootenay Crossing, 12 miles rode, found trail down Simpson and Vermilion very bad.
September 10ᵗʰ - Cold and cloudy
Up and down Kootenay along bank, 18 or 19 miles rode, met B.C. Warden Nixon and Mr. Hope with hunting party.
September 11ᵗʰ - Fair
Down Kootenay River to mouth of Cross River, found fresh signs of Indian hunting camp at mouth of Cross, 17 or 18 miles rode, horse tracks very old.
September 12ᵗʰ - Fine
Down Kootenay River on north side to Cross River, back on east side, found horses near mouth of Cross River, 20 miles rode, met W. McNeil and hunting party.
September 13ᵗʰ - Cold forenoon, warmer afternoon
From Cross River up Kootenay to Wells Ranch Lake on

Upper Kootenay, 23 or 24 miles rode.

September 14th - Fine

Wells Lake to mouth of Ochre Creek, about 20 miles, met B.C. Warden and hunting party.

September 15th -Fine

Mouth of Ochre Creek to Massive, 18 or 19 miles rode, met Phillips.

September 16th - Fine

Massive to Banff on Motor Road, 12 miles rode.

September 22nd - Fine

Got fire pump ready and hose and connection with gasoline, took same to car shed at depot for HES to take to Castle, took lumber to Massive and brought Wood and family to Banff from Healy (shot 1 dog coyote at 9 mile board on Motor Road), 26 miles by auto.

September 23rd - Fine

Bankhead Station and Anthracite, back by way of Upper Road, turned horses out, caught up horse and got him shod for Vick to take to Spray Lakes, 15 miles rode.

September 25th - Cloudy

Getting out supplies and overhauling fire auto, loaded same for Kananaskis, took lubricator to steam shovel at Eldon for McAulay in afternoon, 48 miles by motor speeder.

September 27th - Fine

Got horses from pasture for H.E. Sibbald, helped him pack and went to Mount Edith Pass with him.

October 1916

October 4th - Fine

Took car to stables for Sibbald's pack outfit, turned out horses, took car out with full equipment for fire fighting and got Harmon to take picture, up Motor Road to sulphur spring, 12 miles by auto.

October 6th - Stormy

Banff to Canmore, took lime to Canmore Cabin, also milk bottles to Dr. Atkin at Canmore Hospital, 36 miles by auto and saddle horse.

October 9th - Fine

Packed coal to Observatory on Sulphur Mountain with Wood, 5 six packs, turned horses in pasture when we got to town, 16 miles rode.

October 11th - Fine

Banff to head of Brewster Creek with Deputy Wood and pack outfit with material for shack, 15 miles up creek, 40 miles rode, intended to stay the night at Healy Cabin but some of the pack horses broke for Banff and we were unable to head them off so had to come to town making it a very long day for horses, 15 hours.

October 12th - Fine

Up to yard and around town all day, overhauling car and helping Ford man to fix it, got car running right in afternoon, cause of trouble was water and dirt in gasoline, went to Hot Springs at 9:30 p.m. with Chief Warden HES to try and locate black bear that was doing damage at hotel, saw bear which was a very large one, came home at 2 a.m., 10 miles with auto, 18 hours.

October 13th - Fine

West to Massive with fire fighting outfit to get pictures of outfit when working and tried out fire hose, up to Hot Springs with Wood at night, stayed till 6 a.m. and did not see bear at all, went to Loop on way down, saw about 12 deer, 30 miles by auto.

October 16th - Rain

To pasture for horses, helped Wood and Phillips pack up material for Spray Lake Cabin, went up Spray Valley with them and then to Buffalo Park for saddle horses, 10 miles rode.

October 19th - Fine

Overhauled fire auto in forenoon, Motor Road to Sawback, picked up horse for Sanson for Sulphur Mountain.

October 21st - Snow forenoon, fine afternoon

Loaded up car with brick for Kananaskis but got word from Sibbald not to go so unloaded car again, Motor Road and east along Tote Road to Government Dam, 10 miles rode.

October 23rd

Got outfit ready and took same to pasture, ready to start for Red Deer with horses, left afternoon, went to Stony Creek Cabin, 20 miles rode and by auto.

October 24th - Fine

Stony Creek to Cuthead Cabin with horses, 7 miles rode.

October 25th - Stormy

Cuthead Cabin to Windy Cabin via Cuthead Summit, about 3 inches of snow, 12 miles rode, met Deputy Bevan.

October 26th - Cloudy

Windy Cabin to Red Deer Cabin by Panther River, 30 miles rode.

October 27th - Fine

At Red Deer Cabin all day, helped Bevan gather in horses - removed shoes for pasture on winter range, resting horses, 7 or 8 miles rode.

October 28th - Fine

Red Deer to Windy Cabin, 30 miles rode.

October 29th - Snow all day

Windy Cabin to Banff, 36 miles rode.

November 1916

November 3rd - Rain and snow

Got horses ready for H.E. Sibbald and Rodd for trip to Spray Lakes, rustled up set of runners, mended same and took them for crossing at 7 mile board for Wood, also took rock salt along Motor Road for sheep, met Joe Boyce and Deputies Phillips and Wood.

November 6th - Fine

Banff to Healy Cabin, hauled Wood's outfit to river, 6 trips, brought horses for HES from stables in evening, 15 miles rode and walked.

November 7th - Fine

Packed stuff for Bevan and took same to station, took car to stable, washed car and got Bert Sibbald to adjust and put new carburetor in, 5 or 6 miles walked and auto.

November 9th - Snow all day

Took Jordan's outfit to house, turned horse in pasture, caught up Jupiter for McAulay, took hay to pasture for work horses, 10 miles auto and rode.

November 11th - Cold

Motor Road to Mount Edith Pass, Hot Springs, took rifle to Garrett to get coyote, 15 miles rode.

November 14th - Warmer

Buffalo Park, Motor Road and Moffatt's, up town, set out bait for coyote at mill, got offal from Moffatt's, frozen in ice, 10 miles rode.

November 15th - Fine

Motor Road to 7 mile board, down around mill in forenoon and evening (shot very large male coyote at bait), went up with HES and Harmon to get pictures of sheep, no luck, 18 miles walked and rode.

November 16th - Fine

Down around Moffatt's and sawmill in forenoon, west on track to Sawback east mile board with H.E. Sibbald and Phillips, saw carcass of sheep found by Phillips, skinned out same and found bullet holes in ribs, brought head and front minus shoulders down to Banff by speeder, 16 miles walked and motor speeder.

November 17th - Fine

Down to mill early morning, met Sawback section boss and let him see suspected men, but he was unable to recognize either, put out more bait and removed springs off auto, 6 or 7 miles walked.

November 19th - Fine, strong west wind

Motor Road to Mount Edith Pass, out before daylight after coyotes, met Warren going west, went west with him and Sibbald in afternoon, found carcass of sheep that had been killed, examined same and brought it to town with skull, 12 miles rode, walked and auto.

November 20th - Fine

About town all day, searched Simpson's house for scalp belonging to sheep killed, also got deer meat from Fowles' house where La Casse lives, saw scalp, tried on skull and it matched every cut, visited King Edward ice house and Mitcheltree's for meat, found nothing, 5 or 6 miles walked.

November 24th - Fine

Got horse shod in forenoon, up to CPR Hotel and Spray Avenue, west on Motor Road to Sawback hill, saw two robins - 2 miles and 5 miles west of Banff, 16 miles rode, met James McLeod and he asked J. Warren and myself if we wanted some bait for coyotes and told us to catch some old crippled horses of the Brewster outfit and shoot them off - 5 or 6 in number.

November 28th - Fine

Sundance Canyon, Loop and new moose pasture, down to mill at night and at daylight, took old horse to Sundance Canyon in afternoon, killed off for bait, also killed off a cripple for McCallum in afternoon at Loop, took Rodd through new moose pasture looking for springs, 15 miles walked and rode.

November 30th - Fine, strong west wind

West on Motor Road to Lakes, up Squaw Mountain to Wood's camp, 8 miles walked, saw Ballard and Ward and one other, shot 1 coyote female, wounded large dog.

December 1916

December 7th - Fine

Motor Road and Vermilion Lakes, about town with Fyfe in afternoon, getting count on dogs at large - to summons owners, 10 miles walked, prepared scalp of sheep.

December 8th - Fine

At Police Court forenoon, Motor Road, Lakes and Squaw Mountain, set traps at station for coyotes, 10 miles walked, fed horses.

The Banff Crag & Canyon - December 9th, 1916

Paid Fancy Price for Mutton

James Simpson convicted of shooting Rocky Mountain Sheep within park limits

The police court was crowded Wednesday afternoon

with citizens anxious to hear the trial of James Simpson, charged with killing mountain sheep within park limits.

Magistrate Collison occupied the bench, the crown was represented by Attorney C. Adams of Calgary, the defendant conducted his own case.

The accused was charged by H.E. Sibbald, chief game warden, with three separate and distinct offences as follows: with killing a mountain sheep three and a half miles west of Banff along the Motor Road, on or about Nov. 18th, with unlawfully having portions of a mountain sheep in his possession; with having killed a mountain sheep near the 7 mile post on the Motor Road on or about Nov. 14th. Defendant pleaded not guilty to all three counts.

By mutual consent the first and second charges were tried concurrently.

J.R. Warren, game guardian, deposed to having followed fresh buggy tracks along the motor road on the morning of Nov. 19th, the rig had turned around 3 ½ miles west of town, saw spots of blood on the snow, traced the tracks back as far as the railway crossing where they were lost, went up the road in the afternoon with Sibbald and Peyto, searched the vicinity and found carcass of a dead sheep hidden under a pile of logs, discovered the head 25 yards away under another log pile, the scalp and four legs of the animal were missing, cleaned the carcass and found that the animal had been shot through the heart.

Game Guardian W.H. Peyto corroborated the evidence of the previous witness in regard to finding the carcass and the head, the carcass was very fresh, had evidently not been killed more than a couple of days.

H.E. Sibbald, chief game guardian, gave evidence along the same lines. He proved that Simpson had a wood limit along the Motor Road from the town to Boyce's limit.

Game guardians W.G. Fyfe and C. Phillips testified that on the following Monday, Nov. 20th they in company with Corporal Baker searched Simpson's residence and found the scalp of a sheep and a quantity of wild game meat in the attic. The foregoing witnesses were severely cross-examined by Mr. Simpson. Bert Sibbald, U. La Casse, Hugh Gordon and Wm. Warren were called and testified for the defense.

The third case was then called. C. Phillips, game guardian, testified to having found tracks of a man in the bush along the Motor Road near the 7 mile post on Nov. 14th, later found the carcass of a dead sheep which had been shot and rolled down the mountain side.

Art Bryant, of the 15th Light Horse, testified to having met Simpson near the 7 mile post on the afternoon of Nov. 14th.

The court found Simpson guilty on each of the three counts. As it was his first conviction, the judge imposed the minimum fines - $50.00 and costs for the first and $25.00 and costs each for the second and third offences. The total amounted to $126.00 which was paid forthwith.

Credit is due the game guardians for the manner in which they worked up the cases, establishing a strong chain of circumstantial and direct evidence.

December 11th - Fine

Around town and up Tunnel Mountain, west on Motor Road to Edith Creek, across meadow at three mile board, down river, 18 miles rode and walked, shot female coyote, nearly shot myself in back of head while taking my rifle through window of stable at mill.

December 12th - Fine

Banff to Canmore with Mr. Childe and Collins to survey town around warden's cabin, 30 miles by auto, met Mr. Sibbald.

December 18th - Snow

Motor Road and station, to Bankhead Station, and Devil's Lake after carcass of deer found in cabin at sawmill at lake, accompanied Mr. Sibbald and Deputy Wright, brought carcass to town, 20 miles by auto.

December 19th - Snow

Motor Road and lakes and horse pasture, skinned out carcass of deer in forenoon, trying to locate marks of it having been killed, found that animal had been drowned, helped Brooks get team and saddle horses from pasture and get them shod, few horses in pasture after dark - 10 horses, 8 or 9 miles walked and rode.

December 20th - Cold

Anthracite, Motor Road to Mount Edith Pass, across to Sundance Creek and home by river, helped Warren and

Brooks get started with horses for Red Deer, shot 1 male coyote, 18 miles rode and walked.

December 22nd - Cold

Motor Road and Squaw Mountain, Sundance Creek and Bow River across lakes, 8 or 9 miles walked, saw coyote on Banff Avenue below house, stalked him to Fox Street.

December 24th - Cold, east wind

Down around station and sawmill on Motor Road, 5 or 6 miles walked, found dead coyote that had taken one of my baits several days ago.

December 30th - Cloudy, milder, strong west wind in Banff

From Banff to east Eau Claire camp and government traps, up Spray to see if any goats were coming to salt lick and found they were not coming down, 20 miles rode.

December 31st - Milder

Station and Motor Road to sawmill, shot female coyote at mill, 3 or 4 miles walked, noticed that padlock was missing off bunk house at Jordan's mill when I passed this afternoon.

C.W. Moffatt at dairy. Whyte Museum of the Canadian Rockies. V408 NA86-84.

Banff Avenue 1916. Whyte Museum of the Canadian Rockies.
V573 NA66-419.

Buffalo at Animal Paddock. Whyte Museum of the Canadian
Rockies. V263 NA71-2908.

Norman Sanson at Sulphur Mountain Observatory. Whyte Museum of the Canadian Rockies. V408 NA86-20.

Work horses near Banff.

Nineteen Seventeen

January 1917
January 1st - Fine, windy on Sulphur Mountain
Banff to Observatory on Sulphur Mountain to take readings on thermometers for N.B. Sanson, 14 miles walked and snowshoed.
January 2nd - Cloudy
Helped Warren get outfit ready for Castle and Johnston Creek, packed bears for Ottawa, helped grind axes, shot male coyote at mill, 5 or 6 miles walked.
January 8th - Mild, windy, some snow
To Hot Springs and part way up Sulphur Mountain on way to Observatory but found I had left my key at home, down around station and Motor Road, caught female coyote in trap at mill, 10 miles walked and drove.
January 9th - Mild
To Observatory on Sulphur Mountain and along Motor Road, about 15 miles rode and snowshoeing, had to break trail all the way.
January 10th
Motor Road and Vermilion Lakes, Buffalo Park, went down and saw buffalo with Woodworth, buffalo had lost all use of his hindquarters, 8 or 9 miles walked.
January 11th - Cold, east wind
Down around station looking at trap, up to office and saw Super and got tools ready to butcher buffalo, went out to park with Super and McAulay and Reggie Holmes, shot buffalo, killed him with one bullet, but gave him two more for good measure, thus proving that a buffalo has a vital spot in the head as well as any other animal, 7 or 8 miles rode and walked, helped skin out beast and brought to town, heard that H. Dyer had shot lynx so went and saw him and confiscated his rifle and also carcass of lynx.
January 12th - Very cold
Up at stores all day, cut up animal and got head and hide ready and shipped to W. and Hine, Edmonton, saw lame

deer near house when going home at night, 5 or 6 miles walked.

January 14th - Cold

Down around CPR Station and west along track, up town in afternoon, saw H.E. Sibbald and reported what I had taken from Dyer and he said that we would not prosecute him right away but by all means keep his rifle - 32 long Martin, but if he (Dyer) raised any row he said he would have to prosecute, told me to skin lynx and keep it as the department would want it if the case came to court, 5 or 6 miles walked.

January 15th - Fine

Working on speeder, to John Morrison's funeral, up at yard most of the day, 3 or 4 miles walked.

January 17th - Fine

Motor Road, Mount Edith, Loop and Sundance Canyon Road, across meadows with Dignall, 15 miles rode and motor road, caught large female coyote in trap, mangy.

January 19th - Fine

Along west fence of moose pasture, Tote Road and Squaw Mountain, Motor Road to 7 mile board and up into Mount Edith Pass, 18 or 19 miles rode and walked, shot large male coyote near salt lick on Motor Road, mangy, got letter of congratulations on the Simpson case from J.B. Harkin, Commissioner.

The Banff Crag & Canyon - January 20th, 1917

Ice Palace Under Way - Committees Working Hard

Work started on the construction of the ice palace and maze Tuesday morning and good progress is being made. The huge structure 90 ft. long by 60 ft. wide will ornament the corner of Banff Avenue and Cariboo Street. The front elevation will be 30 feet with towers, battlements and bastions. Inside the palace will be the maze, composed of intricate passages calculated to puzzle those who attempt to thread its windings.

January 29th - Very cold, blizzard, snow all day from north east

Packing for Mrs. Morrison and got team to go to station

with trunks, up at office and storeroom, met Super, and he said he wanted me to go and work on Ice Palace tomorrow.

January 30th - Very cold, snow from east

Working on Ice Palace all day, moved Morrison's effects afternoon.

January 31st - Very cold

Ice Palace all day.

February 1917

February 2nd - Mild, above zero

Motor Road, Mount Edith Pass, Tunnel Mountain and helping Furnell put up wires for palace, 12 miles rode and walked.

February 3rd

To Hot Springs intending to go to Observatory but turned back on account of storm from the east, helping Furnell wire toboggan slide in afternoon, had accident, Furnell's man dropped set of triple blocks from top of light pole about 20 feet onto my head causing cut about 2 inches in scalp, went to hospital and got patched up, 8 or 9 miles rode and walked.

The Banff Crag & Canyon - February 10th - 1917
Local News
    That Walter Peyto is "a tough nut to crack" was proven when a block and tackle used in the ice palace construction fell upon his head Saturday. Another man would have taken the count for a couple of months, but Walter was back on the job the same day.

February 6th - Fine

Loop and Spray, Sundance Canyon, down at mill, tried out gun, cut down some by J. Ballard, shoots fine.

The Banff Crag & Canyon - February 10th, 1917
Formal Opening of Banff's Winter Festival by Mayor Costello of Calgary
    Dr. Costello, Mayor of Calgary, formally opened the first annual winter carnival at Banff, last night in an address

delivered at the ice palace at eight o'clock.

A display of fireworks followed Mayor Costello's address, set off from the roof of the Mount Royal Hotel.

The toboggan slide was in fairly good shape and many visitors and citizens took advantage of it.

At nine o'clock crowds of people wended their way to the Brewster Hall, where the first carnival dance was staged.

February 13th - Mild

Motor Road and sawmill in morning and evening, on river with Rodd trying out horses for ski running, took one in race in afternoon, won first heat, exhibition run for picture men, 4 or 5 miles walked and rode.

February 14th - Fine

Down around mill on Motor Road and lakes, tried out another horse in forenoon, decided to take Major's bay down to run in afternoon and won the cup for Bob Rodd, 6 or 7 miles walked and rode.

February 20th - Cold, east wind

Up town forenoon, down to lower buffalo corrals in afternoon with aliens fixing gates on corrals, 6 or 7 miles walked.

February 25th - Cold

Down around station and sawmill in forenoon, out to Buffalo Park to examine mountain sheep (ram) that Woodworth reported to Mr. Sibbald, skinned out sheep and found him to have broken neck near the shoulder blade, meat too badly bruised so had it burnt, scalp no good, good big heart, 7 or 8 miles walked.

February 26th - Cold

Out to sheep trap putting it in readiness for catching sheep and down to corrals with Woodworth and pulled out three dead elk, 10 miles rode, found Warren's tracks west of Banff where he had been poisoning a carcass in buffalo pasture on my beat.

February 27th - Warmer

West along Motor Road, to lakes and Squaw Mountain wood chute in forenoon, out to park in afternoon, put out some baits for coyote outside sheep fence, went to corral with Warren and cut dead elk for animals at Zoo, 15 miles rode.

March 1917

March 2nd - Cold forenoon, mild afternoon

At Buffalo Park all day, catching sheep, went to station at night, helped out, took down one crate and loaded sheep on express car till 19:30, 12 hours, 10 miles rode and walked, noticed that there was no sign of ticks on the sheep.

March 5th - Fair

West along track, back by Motor Road from 3 mile board, down at Buffalo Park in afternoon examining yak - old bull, apparently his tooth, with HES, Warren and Holmes, 10 miles rode and walked, 9 hours, rode to elk pasture to look at new elk.

March 8th - Fine forenoon, snow afternoon and evening

Banff to Johnston Creek and return, helping hoist stringers for foot bridge, 14 hours, 34 miles by motor speeder and walking.

March 16th - Fine

East on Motor Road, locating line for telephone at Duthil and Cascade Flats, 20 miles by auto and walked.

March 24th - Cloudy

Motor Road to Sawback hill, took stock in storeroom for Dignall, 18 miles rode and walked.

March 29th - Snow

Helping Phillips fix up speeder and took same to car house at station, 4 or 5 miles walked.

March 30th - Snow

East on Motor Road to Carrot Creek with aliens burning brush, 1 ½ hours, too stormy to burn, down at Golf Links in afternoon helping build telephone line - 2 hours, 24 miles by auto.

April 1917

April 5th - Snow

Loaded auto, took fire pump to station and later took

Phillips to station with car, returned CPR wire stretcher, about town, 5 or 6 miles auto and walked.

April 9th - Cloudy

Cave Avenue, Buffalo Park, Sundance Road cutting branch away from telephone line - 3 hours on Cave Avenue, down at elk pasture in afternoon with Woodworth.

April 12th - Cloudy

At government yard painting sign boards for cabins and mixing paint for Kananaskis Cabin with H.E. Sibbald, 4 or 5 miles walked.

April 13th - Fine

Banff to Kananaskis Creek on Auto Road with H.E. Sibbald taking paint for cabin, also distributed wire for telephone west of Canmore, found road in very bad condition, 58 miles by auto, 9 ½ hours.

April 16th - Cloudy, some snow

To summit of Squaw Mountain with Warren trying to get to Forty Mile Creek to burn up big log jam by bridge but snow was too deep to get over, 7 or 8 miles rode and walked.

April 17th - Cloudy

At government yard with Warren painting sign boards for cabins - 3 hours, to Buffalo Park to get McAulay for burst main and brought back two men to Spray Avenue, 12 miles by auto and walked.

April 26th - Cloudy

Getting saddle horse shod, helping Fox fill up sacks with oats for Bevan, took old speeder engine to station, 7 or 8 miles rode and walked.

April 30th - Cloudy

Home on sickness in family.

May 1917

May 1st and 2nd

Home on sick leave.

May 5th

Up at yard getting out camp outfit for J. McKay to take to Johnston Creek, west on track with speeder in afternoon to 6 mile board on Auto Road, fighting fire with Sawback section men where fire had got away while burning right of way, 500 yards long by 75 yards wide, only willows and dry poplar, 15 miles by speeder.

May 7th - Warm

To station and Buffalo Park, took gas to station for speeder, 6 or 7 miles by auto, then took Warren to Buffalo Park, helped Woodworth cut out yak calves.

May 15th - Showery, thunderstorms

Loop and Spray Avenue to Forty Mile and Whiskey Creeks, putting up fishing and park notices, 10 miles rode and walked.

May 18th - Cloudy

Making nesting boxes for birds around museum grounds.

May 23rd - Rain

Banff to Brewster Creek to dry timber with Mr. West, 20 miles rode, saw large grizzly track at mouth of Fatigue Creek.

May 28th - Rain

Banff to Johnston Creek with men, 25 miles by speeder, note: men discussing conscription, heard Warren remark that he would be glad when the government changed - pushed him - he expected more of the other government than he was getting from this one.

May 31st - Fair

Painted sign boards, took Black Boy to stables, Hot Springs afternoon, 7 or 8 miles rode and walked.

June 1917

June 1st - Fine

To end of trail up Cascade Mountain via Squaw Mountain with Mr. Wardle and Joe Boyce looking over trail, 12 miles rode.

June 6th - Cloudy

Up Sulphur Mountain to Observatory with Sanson, took horses to top of first mountain, also stripped all paint off outside of building for Sanson, took picture of trench dug by lightning, 16 miles rode and walked.

June 7th

Down around Golf Links and lower Loop morning and afternoon looking for lame deer that has a can on its foot but could not find it, 15 miles rode.

June 8th - Very windy forenoon, fair afternoon

Loop and Golf Links forenoon, washed fire auto in afternoon and then went to Loop and found lame deer, tried to rope it but was unable to get near enough so had to shoot it as its foot was in bad condition, kept foot as a curio, 12 miles rode.

June 9th - Cloudy, some snow

Went to Loop and brought up deer carcass to the Zoo, about 95 lbs of meat, 6 miles by auto, got out camp outfit, ready for trip to Panther River for horses, left in afternoon and went to Stony Creek Cabin, 17 miles rode.

June 10th - Snow

Stony Creek to Windy Cabin on Panther, 17 miles rode.

June 11th - Snow and hail

Down Panther, 10 miles rode.

June 12th - Cloudy, some rain

Windy Cabin to Stony Creek, then to Banff, 34 miles rode.

June 14th - Warm

Banff to Simpson Summit Cabin with Bill Peyto [Editor's note - Bill was back from World War I duty], struck snow at cabin, 25 miles rode.

June 16th - Fine

Down to pasture with men from Field for horses, took same to blacksmith shop in forenoon, west on Motor Road with same men helping them start horses on trail, one horse came back and more after her about 5 p.m., 12 miles rode.

June 18th - Fine

Helping Phillips and H.E. Sibbald overhaul and try out pumps, also fixed up fire car and got saddle horses from pasture for Wood and two for government camp at Castle, 7 or 8 miles rode and walked.

June 23rd - Fine

Locating new trail up Forty Mile Creek from Squaw

Mountain to Mount Edith Pass, 14 or 15 miles rode and walked.

June 25th - Fine

To Mount Edith Pass with Mumford and McKay in fire auto, trip to station with boards for painter, walked along Motor Road to sawmill and Chinaman's garden, down along track, 15 miles by auto and walked.

June 26th - Fine

Went to yard with horses for Sanson but he did not go, went to station with car for 2 marmots, cleaning bear hide in afternoon that came from Canmore, 10 miles by auto, rode and walked.

June 29th - Cloudy, some rain

Banff to Kananaskis Gateway, sawing up lumber for Canmore and loaded same on car in forenoon, helped put up flagpole at Canmore Cabin, 36 miles by auto.

July 1917

July 1st - Fine

About town, examined several fishermen's catches to see if any had over the limit.

July 4th - Showery

Banff to Johnston Canyon, working on new steps, back by speeder, 26 miles by auto and speeder.

July 8th - Hot

To Loop, to Nuisance Ground twice fighting fire (5 hours) with Chief, pumped water 12 hundred feet and had stream of water 45 feet, 15 miles by auto.

July 9th - Hot

Loop and Garbage Grounds - 3 hours - fighting fires, to Tunnel Mountain where we saw smoke - was two ladies boiling kettle near river bank, to station for barrel of batteries, Sundance Canyon in afternoon with Chief, 20 miles rode and by auto.

July 14th - Very hot

West on track forenoon, in afternoon to Sawback siding getting boat out of river, and went to Healy Lodge for tent with Warren and Phillips, 26 miles speeder and walked.

July 15th - Very hot

About town, put out fire in Mrs. Boswell's yard, sealed carbine for Winchel (prospector) at park livery.

July 16th - Very hot

Sulphur Mountain halfway, Spray Avenue, Loop, took Warren's camp outfit to CPR Hotel, took fire pumps to station, 1 for car shed and 1 for Lake Louise, left pack horse at Hot Springs for Sanson, rode over telephone line across Loop, sealed gun for Ballard - number worn off, sheep head carved on stock at grip, 25 miles rode and auto, got horse shod.

July 20th - Hot, west wind, valley thick with smoke, supposed to come from Golden

At Loop all day pumping water to Garbage Ground, then to Sundance Canyon with HES, saw large black bear in grounds, 20 miles by auto.

July 22nd - Smoky

Banff to Stephen with C. Phillips, took fire pump and hose on speeder, 5 hours fighting fire, returned to Banff at night, noticed burnt pine needles falling while walking along track from Stephen to Lake Louise, apparently coming from south, large fire at Fernie, 80 miles by speeder and train.

July 24th - Hot, smoky

Loop, Middle Springs, Spray Avenue, Sundance Canyon, fixing fire pumps in forenoon, 25 miles by auto, located fire at Sundance - fire under tree at falls - cause picnickers, 3 or 4 feet, no damage.

July 26th - Hazy, hot, smoky

Buffalo Park, up Squaw Mountain, station and Sundance Canyon, 20 miles rode and by auto, sealed carbine for Winchel.

July 27th - Cooler, cloudy, slight rain early morning

To pasture, caught pack horse, took 2 saddle horses and pack to Hot Springs, brought car home, loaded gasoline, cutting branches off trees that obstructed view of Bow Bridge, 10 miles walked, rode and motored.

July 28th - Rain and snow

Fixed fire car in forenoon, to Observatory with telephone in afternoon, got wet through, 15 miles rode.

July 30th - Showery

To lower end of Golf Links and rolled up fire hose and also brought old hose from club house to camp ground for fire practice, then went to camp ground and helped put up tents for Auto Club from Calgary, 10 miles by auto.

August 1917

August 6th - Showery

At Buffalo Park and sheep pasture helping round up animals for J. Keen (movie man), then to camp at Spray with stoves after supper, 10 or 12 miles rode and motored.

August 7th - Showery, snow very low last night

Out to Buffalo Park, helping round up elk for pictures, got chased by old bull, got saddle horse shod in afternoon, 14 or 15 miles rode.

August 15th - Hot

Getting horses from pasture and helping McFadden fix up outfit to get to Spray Lakes, out to Park repairing fence with Warren in readiness for goats if any caught.

August 17th - Fine

Out at Buffalo Park and moose pasture with Mr. Whyte, Hot Springs in afternoon, 28 miles by auto and walked.

August 19th - Hot

Banff to Cochrane to get horses that were lost from Canmore, 40 miles by train.

August 20th - Hot

Cochrane to Horse Creek to get horses to town, 20 miles rode.

August 21st

Cochrane to Kananaskis, 32 miles rode, left one horse with Staple.

August 22nd - Hot

Kananaskis to Banff, 28 miles rode.

August 23rd - Hot

Up Spray Valley to government traps for 4 goats with Chief Warden and Wardens Phillips and Warren, 24 miles by auto and walked.

August 24th - Fine

Out to Buffalo Park to see goats forenoon, up Squaw Mountain in afternoon, then to Eldon at night with Chief to fire that had got away from road gang, 35 miles by auto and saddle horse.

August 26th

West on track to Sawback, found small fire left by fishermen at mile 85, to fire on right of way - this fire was passed up by CPR Fire Warden, 15 miles by speeder.

August 28th - Fine

East on Auto Road to Carrot Creek with HES, took fire pump to river for Phillips to work on, then brought pump back to garage after coming from Carrot Creek, 25 miles with auto.

August 30th - Fair

Packed horse for Mr. Sanson, then to Loop and Buffalo Park, saw large black bear at Garbage Grounds, 10 miles rode.

September 1917

September 5th - Fine

About town, getting outfit ready to go to Red Deer Ranch via Laggan, 5 or 6 miles rode and walked.

September 6th - Fine

Banff to Laggan forenoon, helping Caine make up packs in afternoon, 35 miles by train.

September 7th - Rain and snow

Laggan to Drummond Glacier via Little Pipestone Summit, 25 miles rode.

September 8th

Drummond Glacier to Scott's camp on Red Deer River, saw number of sheep on upper Red Deer near Scott's camp, 30 miles rode.

September 9th - Fine

Scott's camp to Ya Ha Tinda (Brewster's) Ranch, met Wardens Bevan and McKay, 8 or 9 miles rode, shaking out hay.

September 11th - Cloudy

Mowing and stacking hay forenoon, mowing in afternoon, 10 hours.

September 15th - Fine

Up Panther River to Windy Lodge, 12 miles rode, cutting trail, patrol.

September 16th - Fine

Windy Lodge to Banff, ran out of grub, 35 miles rode, 10 hours.

September 19th - Fine

Banff to Castle Mountain over Motor Road, met Warden Phillips at Massive, he went to Castle Mountain with me, took spuds and salt to Castle for Prof. Walcott, west after supper for H.E. Sibbald, then to his house, 6 hours, 38 miles by auto.

September 20th - Rain forenoon, fine afternoon

East on Auto Road to Canmore with George Pickering, 30 miles by auto, out early morning looking for dogs that kept us up at night.

September 21st - Fine, rain forenoon

Out near my house on Banff Avenue, got 2 male dogs and 1 female - 2 males were causing a disturbance every night - scared the rest about to death, west on Auto Road to big meadow with horses to pasture, 12 miles rode and walked.

September 23rd - Fine

About town and to Bankhead Station, 15 miles by auto and walked, saw 2 buck elk fighting in pasture.

September 25th - Fine

Took two horses to office for Mr. Finlayson, got outfit ready to take coal to Observatory, 4 horses came from Field, 2 very thin, one of these almost unable to walk, 8 or 10 miles rode.

September 26ᵗʰ - Very windy

To Sulphur Mountain Observatory with coal (6 packs) for Sanson, 16 miles rode.

September 27ᵗʰ - Cloudy and windy

Helped Warren get team horses from pasture then loaded wagon, went to Bankhead for Wright, took Field horses to pasture - 3 miles west, 20 miles by auto and saddle horse.

October 1917

October 3ʳᵈ - Very windy, showery

Up Spray Valley and then to Buffalo Park, watching breaks in fence, helping Woodworth drive buffalo bull from lower field, 10 miles rode.

October 4ᵗʰ - Cloudy

Up Spray Valley to first camp - 5 miles rode, with feed for forestry camp, Cave and Basin and Healy Trail mending telephone, 22 miles rode and drove, met J. Jackson and son coming to Banff.

October 8ᵗʰ - Fine

Loop and Sundance Canyon Road to Healy Trail, station and Buffalo Park repairing telephone in forenoon and afternoon (5 hours), took Prof. Walcott's camp outfit from depot to Buffalo Park, 15 miles by auto.

October 18ᵗʰ - Cloudy, cold

Double sacked oats for Red Deer, fetched speeder from station, Loop in afternoon with Phillips and Mumford taking down and rolling up wire along trail, 10 miles walked and auto.

October 19ᵗʰ - Snow, very cold

Took speeder to station, west along tracks to big meadows, out to Buffalo Park and inspected mountain goat that died, 10 miles rode and speeder.

October 21ˢᵗ - Snow

West along tracks to big meadows, to Cave Avenue and through bush south of HES house looking for bear that had been bothering around the houses on Cave Avenue, 10 miles walked.

October 22nd - Fine

West along track to big meadow, west on Auto Road to Massive and Johnston Creek with Warden Phillips, brought back tent and stove from Red Cross camp, 36 miles by auto and walked.

October 25th - Fine, snow at night

Buffalo Park, west on track to big meadow, Auto Road to Sawback hill, 18 miles rode and walked, called out 11 p.m. to go to Muskrat Street for a bear that was sitting on a man's doorstep, ran out bear in bush, did not hit him - home 12 p.m.

October 26th - Fine

Out at daylight after bear, together with Phillips looked for bear and caught up with him at Hot Springs. Phillips got one shot at him and he came down through the bush to Spray River, along Tunnel Mountain through bush, went to meadows and brought in bunch of horses to go to Red Deer, 15 miles rode and walked.

October 27th - Snow

Brought horses up from pasture to government yard, branding and numbering them all, 5 miles rode.

October 30th - Fine

Down at pasture in forenoon taking shoes off horses that were to be farmed out for the winter - 3 hours, drove horses to Canmore Cabin in afternoon - 4 hours, 22 miles rode.

October 31st - Fine

Helped Curren and Mumford get started with horses for Kananaskis, then came to Banff - 5 hours, 16 miles rode.

November 1917
November 1st

Packed up carcass of mountain lion and shipped same to Edmonton, also shipped stuff to Morley for J. McKay, then took Mr. Mather and W. Fyfe to Canmore with fish for creeks, put some in Duthil Creek and some in Policeman's Creek, and also in Chinaman's Creek at Anthracite, saw Mumford at cabin, 32 miles by auto, picked up young buck mule deer that had broken his neck against the wire fence around Sam Ward's lot on Marten Street, turned in 36 lbs of meat for the Zoo.

November 9th - Fine

Up Spray Valley on east side to fire guard, returned on west side, west along Motor Road to Mount Edith Pass, 16 miles rode, 8 hours patrol, saw bunch of 14 or 15 rams at hillside meadows near Mount Edith.

November 12th - Fine

To station with horse collars and blankets and sent them to Bevan at Lake Louse by train, 2 hours, working on fire auto - 6 hours, at stables.

November 14th - Fine

Working on fire auto all day with Phillips, 8 hours.

November 18th - Mild, cloudy

Buffalo Park and about town at daylight looking for coyotes and spare dogs, 6 or 7 miles walked, 4 hours patrol.

November 22nd - Fine

Banff to Gap on south side of river, at Canmore with HES, took stores to Warren and Curren at new cabin site, 55 miles by auto.

November 23rd - Fine

Went on Auto Road to Squaw Mountain, took lumber and old crate to park in forenoon, out to Buffalo Park - fixed up crate and put Persian ram in then out with Mr. Sibbald and shipped same at station to Glenbow, 20 miles saddle horse and auto, 3 hours patrol, 5 hours misc.

November 29th - Cloudy

Sundance Canyon Road, Bankhead Station and Dairy, to Upper Anthracite Road, Motor Road, and sawmill, repairing Banff-Canmore line - 2 hours, 15 miles rode and auto, 7 hours patrol, after supper helping put wolverine in crate.

December 1917

December 3rd - Fine

Banff to Massive Lodge and return with load of lumber, saw several bunches of sheep, saw Warden Phillips, 24 miles drove.

December 8th - Snow forenoon, clear afternoon

Up town to government stores, Buffalo Park, down around station, west on Motor Road to 2nd Lake, 6 hours patrol, 10 miles rode, heard of a lynx being in town on Beaver Street.

December 10th - Cold, clear, snow

West on Motor Road to Mount Edith Pass, Cave Avenue and Sundance Canyon - 7 hours patrol, 16 miles rode and drove, shot lynx at Mount Edith Pass, Warren was sore because he had no traps and said if he did not get any he would write a letter to Ottawa, - presume he'd write to Mr. Cory with whom he thinks he has a stand in.

December 12th - Snow

Along west fence of moose pasture to Tote Road, west to Auto Road, to Spray Bridge and Rundle Trail, 6 hours patrol, 8 or 9 miles walked, saw Warren with trap at depot and he said he had to pay for his own traps as he did not seem to be one of Sibbald's pets.

December 14th - Warm, milder, snow

Down to Spray Bridge and Camp Grounds and got my trap that I had set there, had told H.E. Sibbald that I would take it up as Warren was to look after that part of the country. As I was coming out to my horse Warren came along and yelled, "What's the game?" I said, "What do you mean?" He said, "What I say." And as he was so sore I let him think I wasn't taking up my trap, he rode away and I climbed my horse and ran after him and he said, "You want the whole thing, you have the pick of the country and you want to go on everything." I told him to come to the office with me as he would not stop long enough to let me explain why I was down there (to take up a trap that I had there before he put his out), then to Sundance Canyon and Motor Road and Mount Edith Pass, 12 miles rode.

December 15th - Mild

Down around timber back of Moffatt's and sawmill, Buffalo Park in afternoon to skin yak but found him frozen solid and part of his belly eaten by coyotes, so left it so that we could thaw it out, shot mangy female coyote at Moffatt's, 6 or 7 miles rode and walked.

December 17th - Mild, snow

Down to Buffalo Park with Warren and skinned out yak that died on Friday night, found she had her shoulder blade out and her lungs were badly crushed, evidently the others had trampled her as Friday night was a very stormy one and they would all be in the shed, used meat for coyote bait, down around sawmill and Moffatt's Dairy, west on Auto Road to foot of Squaw Mountain, 5 hours patrol, 3 hours misc., 7 or 8 miles rode.

December 19th - Mild

West on track and along Motor Road to sawmill, up to office, down to Buffalo Park, after hide and meat of yak, took some meat to sawmill for coyote bait and the hide to warden's storeroom, 6 hours patrol, 2 hours misc., 8 or 9 miles walked and drove.

December 29th - Rain

West on track to Third Lake, across to Auto Road, back same way, snow very deep away from track with thick crust of ice on top, met Joe Boyce one mile west of Banff, along Cave Avenue to Basin, 6 hours patrol, 6 or 7 miles walking and snowshoeing.

December 31st - Chinook, cloudy, rain

West on Auto Road to Mount Edith Pass, broke trail all the way, Cave Avenue to Sundance Canyon and Healy Trail, down to sawmill and Moffatt's, 7 hours patrol, 18 miles rode, got lynx at pass in trap.

Ice Palace built by World War I alien Prisoners of War - 1917.
Whyte Museum of the Canadian Rockies. V573 NA66-180.

Ben F. Woodworth, Percy Woodworth and Joe Woodworth at
caretaker's cottage at Buffalo Park. Whyte Museum of the
Canadian Rockies. V573 NA66-285.

Nineteen Eighteen

January 1918
January 5th - Fine
Banff to Exshaw and gateway on poaching case and return, 56 miles by speeder and train, got telephone message from Staple last night at 10:30 and another at 12:30 telling me there was something doing in Exshaw and that he knew the men had the meat cached at the powder house. He went and saw it with the night watchman. I intended taking the train down at noon but Fyfe said he guessed we had better both go down. We went on the speeder but did not get there until 3:30, searched Dobson house finding nothing and then went to the watchman's cabin and powder house, seized a 32.55 rifle and 22 belonging to Stevens, and also found 2 carcasses of deer hanging in the powder house, confiscated the bunch. Note: Fyfe was passing himself off as the Deputy Chief Warden and Assistant Superintendent and telling Goodman the watchman that he would use his power to get the judge to be lenient with him, if this man pleaded guilty. Fyfe also went with this man Goodman to see the Super of the cement works to see if he would put up Goodman's fine.
January 7th - Fine
Fixing up fire auto in forenoon and left for Exshaw at 11:00 as Fyfe said he wanted some pictures and to take the summons down - we got no further than the Anthracite hill. I finally rode down leaving Banff at 1:30, 34 miles rode and by auto (saw Staple and Wright).
January 8th - Blowing from east
Kananaskis to Banff, saw Warden Curren at Canmore and rode home with Wright, 28 miles rode.
January 9th - Cold
Sundance Canyon and Healy Trail, Auto Road to summit and at police court hearing deer case, $50.00 and costs each, 15 miles rode.
January 10th - Cold
Along west fence of moose pasture to Tote Road, west to

Auto Road and sawmill, Sundance Canyon, west along track to 3rd Lake, 8 or 9 miles walked and on speeder, cut up deer meat and Fyfe distributed it, over 48 lbs to stores for animals, Barney Collison was upset about not getting a good piece.

January 14th - Cold

West on Auto Road to Mount Edith Pass and Boyce's camp, down to sawmill and east on Tote Road to Forty Mile Creek, along west fence of moose pasture, caught mangy female coyote on Tote Road, saw large number of deer on Auto Road, 12 miles rode and walked.

January 17th - Cloudy

To Sundance Canyon and to Buffalo Park twice to inspect four horned ram that died of old age, took carcass to near sawmill for coyote bait, then took Mr. Sibbald down to Buffalo Park to look over other goats, 16 miles rode and motored.

January 24th - Snow

Over Squaw Mountain on Cascade Trail with Ballard, helped him fetch in his traps and toboggan, no signs of any more wolverine in that country, 10 miles snowshoeing, hard going.

January 26th - Fine

West on track to big meadows and crossed to river and Canyon Road, west on Auto Road to Boyce camp, 12 miles rode and walked, shot female coyote at 3rd Lake, putting out baits and trap for coyotes, found another deer carcass on lake, reported to Chief Warden that coyotes were killing deer along hills north of Auto Road. He told me to get Ballard to help me for a few days. Between us we could think out some way to get the large coyotes that were killing but to give Ballard to understand that he was not to go after them without me, took a ride along Motor Road this afternoon, saw five coyotes but only got one.

January 27th - Fine forenoon, stormy afternoon

Along moose pasture to Tote Road, west on Auto Road to Second Lake and crossed to river and came home down ice and out to log chute on Squaw Mountain with Ballard and set some traps around fresh carcass of deer, home after dark, 12 miles rode and walked.

February 1918
February 4th - Stormy
Along west fence of moose pasture to Tote Road, west to log chute on Squaw Mountain, up river to big meadow and west on Auto Road to 5 mile board (looking for deer reported by engineer to be wounded), found female fawn that had been hit by train, took Sanson to Hot Springs, 16 miles rode and walked.
February 7th - Stormy
Auto Road to Vermilion Lakes, Buffalo Park and sheep pasture in forenoon and afternoon, caught young ram in trap and put in crate, set trap and tried to drive others in but had no luck, 15 miles rode, found large deer - buck deer, brought same to car shed at station.
February 8th - Fine, wind
Vermilion Lakes in forenoon and afternoon, out to sheep pasture rest of day, 2 trips, caught female sheep in afternoon and put in crate, at station at night putting crate on express car, 12 hours, 18 miles rode and walked, took deer carcass to 2nd Lake and poisoned same for bait.
February 9th - Snow all day
Banff to Healy Creek Cabin and Sawback looking for spot to put temporary bridge for snowshoeing, met Warden Phillips at Healy Lodge, had to leave speeder and walk home six miles, 16 miles snowshoed and speeder.
February 18th - Fine
Cleaning elk heads and packing hides with Warren for shipment to Ottawa, west on Auto Road to Mount Edith Pass, 12 miles walked and rode.
February 19th - Along west fence of moose pasture to Tote Road, west along Tote Road to Auto Road and station, west along Bow to Sundance Creek, 12 miles snowshoeing, caught mangy coyote in trap, very poor condition - covered with running sores that stank - male, Fulmer cutting trail on

Tote Road - fallen logs.

February 25th

Crating elk heads forenoon - 3 hours, Loop in afternoon - 3 hours, 2 hours to Don Mathewson funeral, 5 miles walked and drove.

March 1918

March 1st - Mild

To Calgary getting some teeth out, sick leave.

March 4th - Cold east wind, snow

Out to Buffalo Park forenoon with Warren, helped Woodworth with young mountain goat, also brought up carcass of four horned sheep to Zoo, about town in afternoon, at stable fixing horses' feet, 6 or 7 miles rode and walked, took Stanley (son) to doctor to get stitches in his hand - 2 hours.

March 8th - Cold, east wind

Sundance Canyon Creek by Sundance Canyon with J. Ballard, 16 miles saddle horse and snowshoeing.

March 9th - Fine forenoon, cloudy

Auto Road to Second Lake and up Squaw Mountain to Ward's wood camp, 6 miles snowshoeing.

March 30th - Mild

At wardens' garage overhauling fire auto and looking out parts that were needed, west to lakes looking for young deer that was sick, saw four animals, all muddy and skinned about the legs very much, apparently had been cut in the ice while crossing the creek between the lakes on Auto Road, poisoned carcass.

April 1918

April 2nd - Mild

At garage forenoon - 4 hours, west on Auto Road to Boyce's camp and Mount Edith Pass and along hills north of Auto Road, 10 miles rode and walked, 4 hours patrol.

April 12th - Fine

Piling brush on lot near Zoo, cut by Mumford, and burning grass around government buildings, 2 or 3 miles walked.

April 16th - Fine

Canmore Lodge to Gap on telephone line, to Gap after Mr. Sibbald and Vick who took a boat to Gap, 26 miles auto and walked.

April 20th - Fine

Banff to park gateway - moving building, 58 miles by auto, busted radiator on car and had a blow out.

April 27th - Fine

Sundance Trail and Healy Creek, Loop and all over islands in Bow Valley, 18 miles rode.

April 29th - Fine

West on Auto Road to Mount Edith Pass, east to Canmore with supplies and camp outfit for Warren and Curren, repaired telephone line 8 miles east, got horse shod, 36 miles saddle horse and auto.

May 1918

May 4th - Fine

Repaired gasoline tank on speeder, to Fish Hatchery, to sucker spring and hatchery helping Vick catch suckers for polar bear, 10 miles auto and walked.

May 7th - Stormy, some snow

Gathering up material for Caine at Red Deer, at yard all day, up to office and about town, 3 or 4 miles walked.

May 9th - Fine

Around east side of Tunnel Mountain to Upper Anthracite Road and Hoodoos, west on track to mileage 85 looking for deer supposed to have been hit by engine of no. 4 passenger train, could not find any trace of animal having been hurt, was knocked into slough but got out and away, Cave Avenue, 15 miles rode and on speeder.

May 10th - Fine

Healy Creek and Brewster Creek trails to Watrick's camp at Douglas Creek and all over Healy Creek flats, looking at timber (Watrick has about 2500 pieces of timber ready waiting for high water), 25 miles rode.

May 13 **- Cloudy**

Getting outfit and loading up car for east, home afternoon, sick girl, 3 or 4 miles walked.

May 14 **- Fine**

Up to government yard and police corral, put horses in corral forenoon, took horse R26 to Moffatt's, killed and dressed same for Zoo, 541 lbs of meat, turned into stores, 4 or 5 miles rode and walked, child still sick.

May 20 **- Snow**

Banff to eastern limits of park with camp outfit for road gang with McAulay in afternoon, up at yard forenoon loading car, 62 miles by auto, 7:30 got home, brought Harrison and Blake from gateway.

May 27 **- Cloudy**

Banff to Massive and return, moving Phillips' household goods and loading in car, 24 miles drove, 5 hours travel, 10 hours work.

May 28 **- Fine**

Banff to eastern boundary of park to road gang's camp, worked 4 hours putting in posts on telephone line with Bevan, 5 hours travel, took stores and fire pump to camp, 65 miles by auto.

May 29 **- Fine**

Anthracite, Hatchery and Sundance Canyon, to Anthracite with horse, helping H.E. Sibbald get outfit away, took telephone wire off tree on Canyon Road while men cut leaning tree that was going to fall on road, 18 miles rode and auto.

May 31 **- Snow**

Banff to Gap Cabin and return to Canmore Lodge, 27 miles drove, put in phone at cabin, met Bevan.

June 1918

June 3 **- Fine**

East on Canmore Trail putting up pointers, repairing line with Chief Warden, helping Warren - skinned fat out of bear hides from Spray, 25 miles auto and walked, 2 hours putting in posts and repairs on telephone line.

June 10th - Hot, very strong wind around 8 or 9, blew lots of trees down

West along Cave Avenue and Sundance Road to Healy Creek looking for break in line - 4 hours, up Spray Valley to Eau Claire camp looking for 4 men's bodies that were drowned this morning, located the boat bottom up ¼ mile below camp, helped turn it over, 28 miles car and walked - 7 hours.

The Banff Crag & Canyon - June 15th, 1918
Four Are Drowned

None of the bodies of the four men who were drowned last Monday morning just about ten miles from Banff on the Spray River have as yet been found. When four of the employees of the Eau Claire Lumber camp, Thomas Brown, J. P. Erickson, J. Ilush and S. Borkas, were drowned, it marked one of the most horrible tragedies that has occurred in this vicinity for a long time. Five men were crossing the river in a boat to do some work on the other side, a young volcano holding sway over the mountains at the time. The river was swollen with the waters that had come down from the mountain in considerable torrents as a result of the hot spell of the few days previous, and the wind rocked the boat to and fro. It was impossible to control the boat in any way, and this was soon realized by William Webster, the only man who was saved. He jumped out and by some hard swimming reached the shore in safety.

The others stuck to the boat, but it kept filling with water and was soon overturned. The unfortunate men went down for the first time but managed to hang onto the sides of the boat. However the light craft was helpless in the swift torrent and the strength of the men soon gave out. Constable Meagher of the Provincial Police and the member of the RNWMP here did all they possibly could to recover the bodies but without success.

June 11th - Hot

West to Castle Mountain, took pointers along road, had to wait at Mount Edith while culvert was fixed, had to cut 2 fir trees off road at bottom of sand hill - 5 ½ miles west, brought Mr. Wood from Castle to Massive, repaired two washouts, telephone out across Bow River, axle on car broke near sucker spring, 32 miles car, 2 hours - cutting trees and repairing holes where washed out, 3 hours - fixing rear end, after supper scared up Chinaman at sucker hole, got his coat and case.

June 13th - Fine

To lower end of Loop following telephone line - 4 hours, out to Minnewanka in afternoon with fire pump trying to pump out Standly's boat, 5 hours, 25 miles saddle horse and auto.

June 14th

At yard working on fire pump from lake, packed same and shipped to Lake Louise, west to Massive with pointers and also stores and drugs for Wood - found him rather sick, 25 miles auto, clearing out bridge at Massive.

June 19th - Hot

To lower end of Loop following telephone line looking for break, could not get to river, too much water, Upper Anthracite Road to Hoodoos and to Cascade Flats, travelled line, found cable broken across Bow, river running very fast, 16 miles saddle horse and auto.

June 27th - Showery

Banff to Castle, and to Johnston Creek with HES, Mumford and Curren, took Mumford's outfit to Castle, brought Mrs. Wood to Banff to register, took back pointers, had 3 blowouts, 11 hours, 62 miles auto.

June 28th - Rain

At yard fixing up Wright's fire pump, painted old auto plates white for temporary use, 4 or 5 miles walked.

June 29th - Fine

Over Squaw Mountain clearing out trail to summit of Cascade Mountain with Curren, 6 hours, 4 hours travel, 17 miles rode.

The Banff Crag & Canyon - June 29th, 1918
One Body Found

On Saturday last the body of one of the four men who were drowned two weeks ago was found about four miles up the Spray River. This is the first one to be found and was that of Steve Borkas, a young lad of 23 years old. He had been working at Eau Claire lumber mills a short time only when the tragedy occurred.

His father, who has been a resident of Bankhead for some years, came into Banff immediately and the funeral took place the next day, Sunday. The body was barely damaged at all allowing to the iciness of the water.

June 30th - Fine

Down along Forty Mile Creek back of depot and down along creek through moose pasture, saw no one fishing, 5 or 6 miles walked.

July 1918

July 4th - Fine

Loop and Sundance Canyon, shipped oats to Phillips.

July 5th - Cloudy

To Sulphur Mountain Observatory with Curren, repairing telephone line and installing new phone, 8 hours, 14 miles rode and walked.

July 6th - Fine

At park catching Persian sheep and shipping same to station and back after supper with young lamb that was being shipped by mistake, Sundance Canyon and Loop to Eau Claire camp, 25 miles saddle horse and auto.

July 8th - HOT

To Loop getting wire strung across river by Eau Claire boatmen - 4 hours, to Bankhead and Devil's Lake, brought back pump and engine from lake, took Sanson and outfit to Wright's and helped Wright pack up, 25 miles auto.

July 9th - Hot

To Upper Anthracite Road, to Hoodoos and Cascade River and Loop to Bow, repairing Banff-Canmore line - 4 hours, 6 hours patrol, around Camp Grounds, 20 miles saddle horse and auto, sealed carbine for Winchel - Cochrane.

July 12th - Rain

Re-salting horse hide at yard, repairing halters - 2 hours, drove Mr. Sanson to Hot Springs and put new batteries in mountain phone at Bath House, 7 or 8 miles drove and walked.

July 13th - Fine

East on Auto Road to Carrot Creek, met Warden Bevan and repaired Banff-Canmore line between railway and Cascade River - 2 hours, 18 miles by car.

July 15th - Hot

Sundance Canyon, Loop, followed by Forty Mile Creek along through Moffatt's Dairy and up to 1st Lake, 15 miles rode, 4 miles by car, to Alpine Club House after black bear after supper - 3 hours, shot bear just about dark.

July 16th - Hot

Up Spray Avenue to Lougheed's house, pile of brush burning near road, got fire hose and connected with hydrant - 2 hours, no damage, Banff to Castle Mountain with Mumford's outfit, Buffalo Park and Alpine Club, took horses to hatchery, 28 miles by car.

July 17th - Hot

Up Sulphur Mountain to Observatory testing out telephone line in case of fire at Observatory - 3 hours, registered about 12 people while up there, to Alpine Club after supper in McAulay's car, 20 miles rode.

July 18th - Hot

Sundance Canyon, found fire burning in bush by road 2 ½ miles west of Banff, also several small smudges near canyon, came to town and got fire pump and Chief Warden, then drove to fire and put out, started from some picnickers having a smudge and not putting out, impossible to find out who these people might be, burnt about 50 square feet of second growth jack pine, west along Auto Road and Loop, 25 miles by auto.

July 19th - Fine forenoon, rain and thunderstorm afternoon and evening

To Hatchery with horses and packed, then took gasoline and pump to lake, back to Bankhead and put key in shaft, back to lake, with Blake killed horse at park for animals, 4 hours, 25 miles car and horse, went to Hot Springs after supper with Chief Warden, got black bear, brought to town.

July 24th - Fine

Cutting trail in Mount Edith Pass - 4 hours, burning brush on Cave Avenue - 4 hours, took Chief Warden's group to station with Curren, 15 miles rode, walked and auto, saw several sheep ewes and lambs.

July 28th - Fine, hot

Banff to Eldon to old camp with Howard for dynamite, 6 hours patrol, 56 miles by auto.

August 1918

August 2nd - Stormy

West on track to big meadow, level of water was receding - wasn't any on hay field, to park in afternoon trying to put out elk (1 female broke her shoulder in the fence), also caught bull yak and cut his hoofs, 12 miles rode and on speeder.

August 3rd - Rain forenoon, clear afternoon

Rode out to park - too wet, out in afternoon, located elk with broken shoulder - shot and skinned same for Zoo, also ran several into deer field and helped put them out - 5 hours, 10 miles rode, out tonight till 12:45 waiting for bear at CPR pond, nothing doing.

August 6th - Fine

Hot Springs (3 times) and Loop, Camp Grounds to Sulphur Mountain with copper wire, bear broke into Comm. Wilson's house on Spray Avenue, also house on Cave Avenue and into several meat ice boxes, 25 miles rode and walked.

August 7th - Fine

Trailing around after bear who had torn down Garrett's ice box and stole grub from tent at Hot Springs - 10 miles auto, went to Hot Springs again at night and Warren shot black bear that apparently was coming up to where it had torn down the ice box, 16 hours, got home about 1 a.m.

August 9th - Cloudy

Hot Springs and Alpine Club House, Spray Avenue, hunting around trying to run into Mr. Bear that was around Cave

Avenue and Spray Road, 18 miles rode and walked.

August 10th - Cloudy

To Hot Springs at 4 a.m., Camp Grounds, Loop, Spray Valley, Bankhead, auto road to foot of Squaw Mountain and Hot Springs hill after dark, CPR road, to Sibbald's house and set bear trap, 30 miles car and walked.

August 11th - Rain all day

Sunday, home all day, up to Chief Warden's house tonight with bait for bear trap.

August 12th - Cloudy, stormy afternoon

Up Sulphur Mountain with Furnell, putting up lightning arrester along top of ridge, 14 miles rode, 8 hours.

August 14th - Cloudy

Banff to Mystic Lake with Vick and Sanson, 20 miles rode and walked.

August 15th - Showery

After horses - towards Banff and then packed up and brought Vick to Banff, 25 miles rode and walked.

August 19th - Fine

Got horses shod for Bevan, went to Hatchery, got fish for Gap, took horses to Duthil, met Bevan, got out saddle for Wood, 15 miles rode.

August 21st - Showery

To Mystic after Sanson, saw small silvertip on Forty Mile Creek, 35 miles rode.

August 24th - Fine

To Observatory on Sulphur Mountain with Furnell, fixing lightning arrester on top of mountain, 14 miles rode and walked.

August 31st - Fine forenoon, rain afternoon

To Bankhead with brick and cement for Wright, repairing car in afternoon - radius rod, 12 miles by car.

September 1918

September 3rd - Fine

Banff to Lake Louise with horses for Chief Warden - 73 miles saddle horse and train, met Warden Mumford at

Castle and Warden Phillips at Lake Louise, 10 hours.

September 4th - Fine

To station with stuff for Vick to take to Laggan, west on Auto Road to Castle Mountain, took out pointers and helped Mumford repair sign board and pointer at Johnston Canyon that had been broken by someone whom it was impossible to find as this road is used by so many every day, 8 hours, 40 miles by car.

September 5th - Hot

West along Auto Road to Johnston Creek, put up remainder of pointers, also started out after supper with police to go to Johnston Canyon to look for two men that were apparently lost in the bush above canyon, but met the party coming back, 12 hours, 45 miles by car and 12 miles in Brewster's vehicle.

September 9th - Fine

Took horses to pasture, west on Auto Road to Sawback hill, 20 miles rode and 2 miles by car.

September 10th - Fine, hot

Sealed rifles for Pepper and Thomas - Fyfe has number, took Stinson and Fyfe to Exshaw, took oats to Bevan, inspected coal prospect and Chinaman's pig pen, Fyfe gave him orders to clean up in two days, brought luggage from station for HES, 50 miles by car.

September 12th - Hot

Banff to Canmore with fire pump, working on fire back of mines, could not get enough water to put fire out, Bevan got men from coal company to dig around on company land, 20 miles by car.

September 20th - Fine

Banff to Canmore Lodge, went with Bevan out to where fire was smouldering, did not remove fire pump, 35 miles by car.

September 26th - Fine

Hot Springs, Sundance Canyon Trail, along hills between Banff and Anthracite, met Bevan and Staple at Anthracite with horses, 12 miles car, 10 miles rode.

September 28th - Fine

Banff to Castle Mountain with supplies for Mrs. Mumford, getting horses from pasture and putting others in from stables, 40 miles car and rode.

September 30th - Fine

Catching up horse and killing same for Zoo at horse pasture, Loop and Spray to Hot Springs, 15 miles rode, sealed rifles for Fred Pepper - Savage and Winchester.

October 1918

October 1st - Fine

Banff to Spray Lakes with supplies for hatchery, stayed overnight in government cabin, 50 miles drove.

October 3rd - Cloudy

Helped unload work horses off car, took same to east side of Tunnel Mountain, returned saddle to hatchery, looking around Camp Ground, 10 miles rode and car, sealed gun for Amoss.

October 4th - Fine

At pasture catching up horse and colt, brought same to stable, to Loop in afternoon, 15 miles rode, sealed gun for J.J. Brewster.

October 8th - Fine

East on Auto Road to Duthil, met Bevan with D1 work horses that had got away from Banff, one team of greys missing, went around east side of Tunnel looking for same, no luck, 20 miles rode.

October 10th - Fine

Banff to Stony Creek Cabin with Wright taking D1 workhorses to Red Deer, 17 miles rode.

October 11th - Rain all day

Stony Creek to Windy Cabin on Panther River with horses, 15 miles rode, met Caine at Windy Lodge.

October 12th - Fine

Windy Lodge to Banff and brought 5 head of cripples from Stony Creek to Banff, 32 miles rode.

October 13th - Showery

Took horses up west to 5 mile board, to pasture and went to Buffalo Park with Chief Warden and Warren to get elk out of wire and to see if the other one that was dead was any good to feed animals, 15 miles rode and auto.

October 15th - Cool

West on Auto Road to move horses with Curren and Warren, to park and killed horse for Zoo, went west again to fix fence in pasture, 20 miles saddle horse and auto.

October 16th - Rain, fair afternoon

Banff to Gap with Chief Warden and two men, met Wardens Bevan and Staple at Deadman's Lodge, repaired phone line, 45 miles by car.

October 19th - Showery

Banff to Massive twice, met two B.C. Police 5 miles west of Banff going to B.C., caught Chinaman fishing with nets, 48 miles by car.

October 20th

Banff to Canmore Lodge with supplies for trail gang, caught 3 Austrians stoning a fool hen.

October 24th - Fine

At Police Court (2 hours) forenoon, on game and fish cases, three Austrians fined $1.00 and costs each for stoning partridge, Kwong Chung fined for fishing with nets at sucker springs, Loop and Spray Valley.

October 27th - Fine

About town and getting doctor for Mrs. Curren, splitting wood, getting medicine from drugstore and meeting train at night, 5 or 6 miles walked.

October 29th - Fine

Killed horse for Zoo - one eyed Riley, helping load up meat, west on Auto Road to sucker spring, 8 or 9 miles rode.

November 1918

November 6th - Fine

West on Auto Road forenoon to Sawback hill with Chief Warden after pictures of sheep - with car, saw Joe Boyce cutting logs at 5 mile board, up along Auto Road in evening, 20 miles car and horse.

November 8th - Fine

West to Sawback hill looking for sheep, stopped and spoke to Joe Boyce who was cutting wood near 5 mile board on Auto Road, noticed ravens around on hill nearby, Joe Boyce rode to town in car with me, killed horse for Zoo, accompanied by Warden Warren went west to Boyce's wood limit and after watching ravens awhile found the carcass of Rocky Mountain sheep (ram) that had been shot, no snow to track, forequarters and strip along side of back and under cut, and scalp had been taken away, notified Chief Warden and next morning he went with Warren and me to spot and took pictures.

November 9th - Snow forenoon, fine afternoon

With Chief Warden and Warden Warren I went west to sand hill near Boyce's limit and brought down head of sheep, but not proof of who was killing sheep.

November 10th - Snow all day

On Auto Road at different times during day, no one on road whatever.

November 11th - Fine

Woke at 2 a.m. by fire bell, announcing PEACE, went up town and celebrated with the crowd, had car in parade in afternoon, hauled wood for fire at night, 20 hour celebration.

November 12th - Fine

Banff to Massive Cabin with Wood who had brought his horses to town, met Boyce and Joe Butterworth going west near 2nd Lake, brought back stick of timber with blood marks, 24 miles by car.

November 13th - Fine

Went to Sawback hunting over hills with Boyce and Fyfe looking for what the ravens were eating, 16 miles car and walked.

November 19th - Fine

Auto Road west to 7 mile Sawback hill with Sibbald and

Fyfe wandering around up where sheep was killed - taking pictures, down around Moffatt's Dairy and to Squaw Mountain chute, shot mangy coyote, 18 miles walked and motored.

November 20th - Fine

Up to office forenoon making out statement re: sheep and Boyce, west on Auto Road to 7 mile hill, put seizure notices on 2 piles of wood taken out by Boyce, 14 miles by auto, shot female coyote near dairy.

November 23rd - Fine

Putting crown gear on car, west on Auto Road to Sawback hill with H.E. Sibbald taking pictures of sheep, Sundance Canyon and Healy Trail, 22 miles auto.

November 27th - Cloudy

West to Massive working on well and turning creek so that water would not flow into well, Banff to Canmore with nurse for Mrs. Bevan, 52 miles by auto.

December 1918

December 4th - Snow

Out to park in afternoon, helping Woodworth move domestic sheep and yak bull, 5 miles rode.

December 10th - Fine

Along Tote Road to Squaw Mountain, west along Auto Road to 6 mile board with Warden Wood, saw a few sheep near sucker spring, met McCormick with tourists at 4 ½ miles, saw Geo. Gallop cutting wood at 3 mile board.

December 13th - Fine forenoon, snow afternoon

To Mutch's wood camp on Brewster and by Healy and Brewster Creek Trail with Fyfe and police constable, 24 miles rode.

December 16th - Fine

West to Mount Edith Pass and Vermilion Lakes to Squaw Mountain and around by graveyard looking for signs of anything having been shot as a shot was heard in that direction on Saturday night, 14 miles rode, found the remains of young buck deer near sulphur spring up path, fallen while jumping large logs on side hill, put out baits.

December 18th - Fine

Took car from stable to garage and took off tires and crated fire pump to ship to Montreal, up around Vermilion Lakes, shot female mule deer with leg broken at government house, took meat to Zoo, about 40 lbs, used offal and head for bait, 7 or 8 miles walked and rode.

December 19th - Fine

Took offal of deer up to Vermilion Lakes, dragged same along Auto Road to attract coyotes, 10 miles rode.

December 24th - Fine

Got horse from mines at Bankhead, left same at Bevan's, came back to Banff, 16 miles rode.

Fish Hatchery. Whyte Museum of the Canadian Rockies.
V263 NA71-3448.

View of Castle Mountain from Johnston Creek Bridge - 1921.
Whyte Museum of the Canadian Rockies. V263 NA71-4629.

Deer in Banff.

Nineteen Nineteen

January 1919
January 3rd - Fine
Banff to Healy Lodge via Sundance Canyon to Healy Trail, 12 miles drove, took Bill Peyto and his outfit to Healy Lodge, met Mutch going out to his camp.
January 4th - Fine
West on Auto Road to Mount Edith Pass and 6 mile sand hill, sighted a north and south line from mileage 86 through Boyce's limit, found spot where carcass was found to be outside line - to west about 300 yards, along west fence of moose pasture to Squaw Mountain and Tote Road, along Tote Road to Auto Road and Moffatt's Dairy, 15 miles walked and rode.
January 6th - Fine
West on Auto Road to Mount Edith Pass, up Squaw Mountain to Ward's limit, saw Mutch cutting firs (green) on face of mountain, also found carcass of sheep (ewe) lying in water course, killed by wolverines, set traps around same, 15 miles rode.
January 14th - Fine
West on Auto Road to Boyce limit and Sawback hill and up Squaw Mountain to head of chute, 16 miles rode and walked.
January 20th - Fine
West on Auto Road to 6 mile sand hill, over on south side of track to where Mutch is cutting boom timber, to Mount Edith Pass and Squaw Mountain, 16 miles rode, 8 hours patrol.
January 29th - Fine
Along west fence of moose pasture to Tote Road and Squaw Mountain, up Squaw Mountain to Ward's cabin, 10 miles snowshoeing and driving, Hot Springs in afternoon - repairing Sulphur Mountain line - 4 hours.
January 30th - Fine
West on Auto Road to Mount Edith Pass, saw Sanson's

snowshoe tracks going up into pass, saw J. Edwards cutting timber at mouth of pass, Cave Avenue and Sundance Canyon Road to Healy Trail, 15 miles rode.

February 1919
February 5th - Fine
Up Squaw Mountain to top of chute, walked up to where B. Ward was skidding timber, also walked along snowshoe trail towards Forty Mile Creek, out to Buffalo Park in afternoon, skinning out male elk head and cutting up meat for Zoo, 10 miles rode and walked.
February 7th - Fine
Through moose pasture to Tote Road and west along side of Squaw Mountain to Auto Road, west on Auto Road to Mount Edith Pass and 6 mile sand hill. Saw Mutch and gang loading logs and James Reid and party driving, 15 miles rode or snowshoeing.
February 14th - Fine
Ran in pony ski racing on river with Warren and Holmes, to Sundance and Healy Trail in afternoon, 10 miles rode.
February 20th - Snow
Squaw Mountain to top of log chute, west on Auto Road to Mount Edith, saw Fyfe and Mutch driving west to near sucker spring, also saw Mutch's team hauling to town, picked up pygmy owl and gave to Sanson, 12 miles rode.
February 24th - 30 below
About town and snowshoeing through bush and heavy timber behind Moffatt's Dairy, saw large number of mule deer in timber, 2 or 3 miles snowshoeing.

March 1919
March 7th - Mild
West on Auto Road to Sawback hill, broke trail from sucker spring west, took Warren along trying to locate big ram, 14 miles drove.
March 11th - Mild till 5 p.m., temperature dropped suddenly
West on tracks to river, crossed lakes to Auto Road on

coyote tracks, up to office with diary, east on track to Buffalo Park crossing, 5 or 6 miles snowshoeing and walking.

March 14th - Fine

Moffatt's Dairy and Squaw Mountain, west on Auto Road to Boyce's camp, saw a few sheep near Mount Edith, got out salt and hay for sheep, 14 miles drove and walked.

March 18th - Fine

West on Auto Road to 2nd Lake, Loop to club house, 7 or 8 miles rode, trails very heavy, saw robin at S. Cobb's house.

March 19th - Fine

Through moose pasture to Tote Road and Squaw Mountain, west on Tote Road to Moffatt's and station, west on tracks to big meadow, back across Lakes, 6 or 7 miles snowshoeing, summoned to court as witness in Williams and Prosser case.

March 20th - Fine

At stable forenoon handling colts, 4 hours, at court in afternoon and evening as witness in Williams and Prosser case, 2 till 10 p.m.

March 22nd - Fine, warm

East to steel bridge at Anthracite, at stable in afternoon, halter breaking two colts, 10 miles rode and walked.

April 1919

April 3rd - Fine

Subpoena to be at Calgary Criminal Court all day.

April 4th - Fine forenoon, rain afternoon

At Criminal Court all day, to Banff at night.

April 7th - Fine

West on Auto Road to Mount Edith Pass, caught wolverine, at park in afternoon, examined elk that Woodworth had found dead, cut off head, remainder of carcass not fit to feed to animals at Zoo, apparently been dead for some time. I would say by the appearance of matter running out of neck that it had large abscess on throat, Warren and I burnt up carcass, note: on examining mouth there was nothing to show that this animal had ever had the usual two tusks in lower jaw as there were no holes even supposing them to have been stolen, the head had six spikes on each horn, 14 miles rode.

April 9th - Fine

Washing colts with Creoline - for lice, the colts are supposed to have been fed and looked after by stable boy, and got some hay that was fed to other horses, west along Auto Road and up Squaw Mountain in afternoon, 4 or 5 miles walked.

April 12th - Fine

Buffalo Park and stable, to park after 4 horned sheep, skinned same and took meat to Zoo - 3 hours, washing colts with Creoline and clipped larger of the two - 4 hours, 5 miles drove.

April 15th - Fine

West on track to Johnston Creek with Bill Peyto and Warren to work on canyon, 26 miles by speeder, saw 4 goats - 6 ½ miles west, left rifle with Bill Peyto.

April 16th - Fine

Government stores, Fish Hatchery and station, helped Warren take horses to hatchery and pack up in forenoon, putting tires on car etc. at garage, 4 or 5 miles rode and walked.

April 19th - Fine

About town forenoon, west on track to Johnston Canyon with Chief Warden, took dynamite to camp, 30 miles by speeder, saw large bunch of rams on 6 mile sand hill - Auto Road near track.

April 24th - Rain

West on Auto Road to sawmill and followed creek down through by Moffatt's Dairy to east end of railway yards, 4 or 5 miles walked, shot female coyote near sawmill, saw several deer near Moffatt's.

May 1919

May 6th - Fine

Off duty forenoon, west on track to ½ mile west of mileage

85 watching river in afternoon and evening at fishing holes, men of Mutch's camp suspected of fishing, 12 miles walked and speeder.

May 14th - Warm

Working on beaver pasture - 6 hours, at fire on Loop - Garbage Ground, brought pump from Hot Springs, Auto Road to sucker hole after suckers with HES, heard 2 shots on hillside, caught Malcolm Amoss with Luger, confiscated same and brought Amoss to town, he was tried by Mr. Collison and fined $25.00 and costs, also Joe Blair who was driving Amoss' car was fined as an accomplice $5.00 and costs, home 10 p.m., 4 miles walked, 28 miles by auto.

May 19th - Fine

To Bankhead and east on Canmore Road to 11 mile board to meet Bevan and help bring work horses to Banff, took camp outfit, 10 miles auto and 22 miles by horse.

May 20th - Fine

Lake Minnewanka and west to Johnston Canyon, took Vick to lake, 48 miles by auto, took supplies to canyon.

May 21st - Fine

At yard making rails, west on Auto Road to Johnston Canyon and Castle Mountain, 40 miles by auto, picked up deer on lane between Otter Street and Grizzly Street, appeared to have been poisoned, opened same and found this animal had its insides busted as if it had been hit with a car or had a fall, also 2 ribs cracked.

May 22nd - Fine

East to 11 mile lake, helped Bevan kill horse and brought meat to Zoo, west to Johnston Creek and brought in Watrick and outfit, went to station at night after beaver, took same to pond in Zoo, 57 miles by auto.

May 23rd

Took crate to station and shipped to Ontario, to Bankhead and Lake Minnewanka to inspect log jam on bridge reported by J. Standly, took men out in afternoon, and then went to Loop, 40 miles by auto.

May 24th - Fine

Working on beaver pasture forenoon, Canmore Lodge in afternoon and Sundance Canyon in evening, 38 miles by auto, Mr. Vick also cut poplar and brush for beaver.

The Banff Crag & Canyon - May 24th, 1919
The Pesky Mosquito

An effort will be made by the Parks Department to suppress the mosquito nuisance this year, and the people are asked to assist as by cooperation only can results be attained.

Still water is the natural breeding place for mosquitoes, therefore keep all water utensils covered tightly especially at night, pour coal oil on stagnant pools and see that the back yards are clean and sanitary.

May 27th - Cloudy

Putting coal oil for mosquitoes about town and Loop, Cave Avenue and west to 5 mile board, 20 miles auto.

May 29th - Rain afternoon

Lake Minnewanka loop and station, Fish Hatchery, took fish to lake, also removed deer from side of road on loop, 25 miles by auto.

May 30th - Fine

Took horses to lower buffalo pasture in forenoon, to Johnston Canyon in afternoon, brought back forge and anvil, also pulled out sheep from creek that had come over falls, 5 miles saddle horse and 32 miles by auto.

June 1919

June 1st - Fine

Home all day, moved back into own house.

June 2nd - Fine

Took colt to park and brought back two pack horses in forenoon, went to park with Chief Warden and castrated two colts, 11 miles saddle horse and car.

June 3rd - Fair

To Moffatt's and Buffalo Park, out on Auto Road to small fire, west on Auto Road to 3rd Lake, took horses to Buffalo

Park for Moffatt's, to be killed for Zoo - killed and dressed one, 1 hour on fire, put under control by Gus Johnson, 10 miles rode.

June 4th - Fine

Cutting up old pipe at government yard for use in beaver pasture in forenoon, took car to garage, to Buffalo Park in afternoon, caught up colt and pulled out porcupine quills from his nose, also brought in 3 horses from lower pasture, 10 miles rode and walked.

June 7th - Fine, windy

West on track to 1 mile east of Sawback fighting fire with Wood, 4 ½ hours, 18 miles speeder and walked.

June 11th - Showery, fine

Oiled up new car MV51, took Vick to sucker hole after suckers for Zoo, 10 miles auto and walked.

June 17th - Fine

To Buffalo Park and station six times hauling yak on car for Wainwright, 13 hours, 30 miles by auto.

June 19th - Fine, very warm

At stables painting fire auto in forenoon, west on Auto Road to 3rd Lake and Boyce's camp, 10 miles rode.

June 20th - Very hot

At Bankhead twice in forenoon, out with Sanson putting coal oil out to kill mosquitoes, chiefly on CPR property, 5 miles saddle horse and 20 miles by car, went to 2 mile board to small fire reported by Slim.

June 21st - Hot

East to Canmore Lodge after Bevan to go north for HES, also packed up camp and shipped to Jasper Park, gave Holmes' mare to Bevan, only had one horse in - Mumford's mouse coloured, 35 miles by auto.

June 24th - Hot

East on Auto Road to Kananaskis and park boundary and up into hills to where fire was located on Indian Reserve - 1 ½ miles from park line, came back and reported to Supt., west at night to fire 2 miles east of Lake Louise, took up fire pump, 10:30 - started in fighting fire, 104 miles auto, saddle horse and train, 10 hours patrol, 2 ½ hours fire fighting.

June 25th - Very warm

Still fighting fire, 19 hours fire fighting, fire burned about 85 acres.

June 27th - Showery

Fixing fire auto and drying hoses, took outfit of supplies to Bankhead for Wright and Caine, 8 hours, 10 miles by auto.

June 30th - Rain

Banff to Kananaskis and park boundary with grub for fire fighters - till 11 p.m., 70 miles by auto.

July 1919

July 1st - Fine

About town forenoon, to lower buffalo pasture in afternoon, caught 2 horses for Walcott, 8 miles walked and rode.

July 2nd - Fine

East on Auto Road to Kananaskis and park boundary with pumping unit and hose etc. fighting fire in afternoon and night on park line - 1:00 till 12:30, 44 miles by fire auto.

July 3rd - Hot

West from Kananaskis to road camp 1 ½ miles west of Gap for gasoline, back to park boundary till 7 p.m., camp to Banff at night - 11:30, 60 miles fire auto.

July 4th - Hot

At yard drying out hose and rolling up some dried hose, to Sundance Canyon in afternoon - small fire caused by picnic fire - 1 hour, McAulay, Holmes and myself, 12 miles auto and walked.

July 5th - Hot

At office making out fire report and report on mare that died - one ridden by Bevan to Stony Creek, Sundance Canyon, Forty Mile Creek, Moffatt's and Garbage Grounds, 18 miles walked and rode.

July 7th - Fine

About town, west on Auto Road, Spray Avenue, falls and to swamp behind Camp Ground with Sanson putting out coal oil (done great job today), 10 miles auto (MV51) and walked.

July 12th - Hot, showery

Canmore Lodge to fire fighting, returned to Banff, to CPR Hotel and Military Camp and Fish Hatchery and Tunnel Mountain, took Sanson out with coal oil for mosquitoes, 33 miles by fire auto.

July 15th - Fine

Washed up black car in forenoon and tightened up same, took it to station for Phillips, west on Auto Road to Boom Lake and took names of parties fishing at lake, 68 miles auto (MV51).

July 16th - Fine, very strong wind

To Loop forenoon and afternoon, took 2 men to fight fire at Garbage Grounds, ran out to fire at Canmore, left pump and outfit, returned for men, fire broke out again at Loop, out till 3 a.m., 40 miles fire auto.

July 17th - Cloudy, showery

To Canmore Lodge with fresh gang of men to fight fire, brought back part of night gang, back at night for men, at Loop fire 4 a.m., at Recreation Grounds and fixed pump, with F. Pepper in afternoon, 70 miles fire auto.

July 19th - Fine (Peace Day)

Oiled up fire auto and black car and went to lower pasture with Warren for pack horses and helped F. Pepper away with pack horses for Vermilion Pass, 8 miles rode and walked.

July 20th - Fine

West on Auto Road to Castle Mountain with supplies for highway engineers, helped F. Pepper pack up, 10 miles auto (MV51).

July 21st - Fine

To Canmore Lodge with pump and gasoline for Bevan, to Loop and west to Johnston Creek, took grub to two road camps and Wood, 52 miles auto (MV51).

July 25th - Showery

Killed horse for Zoo and to Canmore Lodge - took plaster for Curren and parts for pump and oil to Bevan, auto

MV51.

July 28th - Fair

Cave Avenue, Buffalo Park, Auto Road to Forty Mile Creek, to station at night, took Mrs. McConnell's outfit to CPR Hotel and put up tent with Warren, 12 miles auto (MV51).

July 31st - Fair

Loop, Camp Grounds, Cave Avenue, and Sundance Canyon putting up fire notices, to station, teaching Warren to run fire auto, also shipped beaver trap to Golden - E. Robinson.

August 1919

August 1st - Fair

West on Auto Road to 3 mile board and down across creek to meadows and to Buffalo Park after trunk with Warren, 12 miles rode and auto.

August 2nd - Fair

Took trunk to station and freight and bags to Fish Hatchery, Cave and Basin, to pasture for pack horse for Rodd, shot T. Faulkner's dog.

August 6th - Cloudy

Took Stewart around Tunnel Mountain Drive in afternoon, skinned out elk head and scalp and salted same, drove Fox to CPR Hotel for oil, took trap to Lady MacDonald's bungalow and set for mountain rat, 8 miles fire auto, 3 miles walked.

August 7th - Fine

Took box to office for Sanson, and to Cave Avenue twice, east to Duthil, put in post for telephone line, 2 hours - telephone, packed windows and nails and shipped to Phillips, 12 miles auto.

August 8th - Hot

Up to office and down near sawmill and killed Brewster horse, also skinned out work mare that died in stables and sent meat to Zoo, hauled up meat from Brewster horse in car, west on Auto Road to 7 mile spring, tried out telephone line, 20 miles auto and walked, 4 hours misc., 4 hours patrol.

August 11th - Fine

Put speeder together and ran west as far as big meadow, to Cave Avenue, Loop, also to Canmore Lodge for Chief Warden, 32 miles black car, 5 miles fire auto, 2 miles speeder, inspected wolf and cut out part of internal organs for analysing.

August 12th - Cloudy

To Bankhead with S. Muir in forenoon - gathered up Curren's outfit and to Bankhead, then Canmore Lodge with Muir and Curren's outfit, 53 miles auto (MV51).

August 13th - Showery

To Buffalo Park, turned out horses caught up for engineers, to Vermilion Summit with Chief Warden and Warden Brooks, took outfit to cabin, 62 miles auto, 10 miles saddle horse.

August 16th - Hot

Repaired radiator on fire auto and took stove and stores to Vermilion Summit Cabin for Warden Brooks, also picked up supplies for engineers at Castle and took same to summit, 62 miles fire auto, putting new spring on fire auto at house after supper - 2 hours.

August 18th - Cloudy, still smoky

Visited Indian campers on Forty Mile Creek and found out where they are going, David Big Stoney and Tom Two Young Men, going over the Vermilion prospecting, had one rifle sealed by Staple, I informed them that the park extended along the road west of the summit, I took Fyfe to Canmore Lodge and met him at night at Carrot Creek Bridge, took fire notices to Bevan, 50 miles fire auto.

August 19th - Cloudy, very smoky

Cave Avenue to fire behind Dr. Lafferty's house, connected up our hose to hydrant and put out for them, to Loop, west on Auto Road to Sawback, tried out line on Sundance Road in afternoon, and rolled up hose, fixed tail light on fire auto, 30 miles fire auto.

August 20th - Hot

Notified Warden Warren that Observatory was open, fixed phone in Chief's office, repairing pump, got radiator soldered and gas tank and pump, took Wright to lake with gasoline, 18 miles fire auto.

August 23rd - Smoky

To lower buffalo pasture and up Spray Valley on east side to Steffanson's camp, took up horse for his use, up trail from hotel to Hot Springs and back by Middle Springs, 15 miles rode.

August 25th - Cloudy and smoky

To lower pasture, caught pack horses and up Spray Valley after Sanson's camp outfit, 28 miles rode.

August 27th - Fair

To office, CPR stable and Loop to Garbage Grounds, shot dog for G. Noble, to Buffalo Park after horse that got loose from stable, to Brewster's office and sealed eleven rifles, shot lame coyote at Zoo and to camp on Squaw Mountain - sealed two rifles for party guided by Phil Moore - Enfield and Winchester.

August 29th - Fine

Up to office forenoon, Hot Springs and Cave and Basin with Horsfall for money, overhauling black car in afternoon, 10 miles auto and walked, sealed 4 rifles - Winchester and Mauser (Potts' party), 2 Winchesters (Mr. Blair's party).

August 30th - Fine

Got car ready for Chief to go to Kananaskis and Morley, to station, west on Auto Road to Mount Edith Pass with horses for Col. Smith and Supt. Wardle, about town, and up again to bring them home, 24 miles car and rode.

September 1919

September 2nd - Fine

About town forenoon, drove to Massive to get horse and brought back load of junk for Wood, got Tex to run in horse, 28 miles car.

September 3rd - Fine

West to Massive and helped Wood to kill horse for Zoo, brought same to Banff, crated fire pump and shipped complete unit to Pincher Creek for Waterton Lakes by express, 28 miles auto.

September 5th - Showery

To Loop hunting for horse lost by Mr. Steffanson, found same and brought to Banff - 5 hours, got him shod and took him to Steffanson's camp, 14 miles rode.

September 6th - Showery

West on Auto Road to shack on Vermilion Summit, brought Warden Brooks to Banff, met Warden Mumford at Castle and Jack Thomas and party hunting in B.C., 62 miles auto.

September 8th - Fine

To Hot Springs and Loop to Garbage Grounds in forenoon, took nozzle to Garrett, to lower pasture with Brooks, moved two colts from west field to lower pasture, also caught mare for Curren to ride, 12 miles car and 8 miles riding.

September 9th - Fine

To Hot Springs with Sanson, to moose pasture, hunted out four horses and caught up two horses for Brooks, to Canmore Lodge with Latam with stove and moved boxes from Canmore Station to Lodge, 37 miles black auto, 2 miles saddle horse.

September 13th - Fine

To Buffalo Park and mountain sheep pasture, west on Auto Road - 1 mile west of Sawback with Mr. Cornelius Vanderbilt and party of moving picture men taking mountain sheep picture of hunting scene, 35 miles auto and walked, 8 hours patrol.

September 17th - Fine

Prince Arthur of Wales in Banff, made "Chief Morning Star" of the Stoney Indians, station, Buffalo Park to race track, west on Auto Road to Hillsdale with beef for government camp, saw Wood, saw 3 female sheep at sulphur spring, 32 miles auto and rode, 7 hours patrol.

September 18th - Fair, windy and cloudy afternoon and evening

Cave Avenue, station, east on Auto Road to Canmore Lodge and around office, got orders from Chief (who had to go east) to stay around office to register parties and seal guns until Warren returned, sealed several guns and took gun seals to Warden Latam at Canmore after supper, guns sealed: M. Carpentier - 2 rifles, F. Jordan and party - 4 rifles, Capt. Calder - 1 rifle - Mauser and Luger pistol, 3 hours patrol, 9 hours misc., 30 miles auto and walked, sold hunting licences to F. Phillips and E. Carpentier.

September 19th - Showery

At office (Chief Warden's), and to Garbage Grounds in afternoon, 1 hour with Mr. Blair trying out rifles, at garage and patched 3 inner tubes, sealed 2 rifles for Mr. Blair, Malcolm Amoss - 1 rifle - Mannlicher, sold hunting licence to Amoss, 10 miles walked and motor.

September 23rd - Fine

Carrot Creek with Sanson, to Canmore and Gap road camp to get steamroller man for McAulay and took government grub to Canmore Lodge for Brooks, Kananaskis, saw Latam 2 miles west of Canmore, 48 miles auto.

September 28th - Fine

Buffalo Park and Tunnel Mountain Road, took loaded rifle from Dr. Walcott's packer when riding by my house, received telephone message from Phillips at Lake Louise to go up with pump in morning, 3 miles walked.

September 29th - Fine

Banff to Temple and Lake Louise at night then to Banff, fighting fire, fire 2 miles east of Temple - with Phillips, 7 hours, 50 miles train and walked.

October 1919

October 2nd - Fine

Buffalo Park and upper meadows and blacksmith shop and garage, returned Walcott's gun taken from his packer, 8 miles saddle horse, 5 miles car.

October 5th - Fine

To Cave Avenue and station with HES in forenoon, Mr. Walker phoned at 2:30 of fire in meadows, told Warren, could not get McAulay, went to fire with buckets and sacks, unable to check in grass, took pump up in locomotive, ran till 12:00, 1 stack of hay, 5 or 6 tons burnt, 15 miles auto, speeder, walked.

October 6th - Fine

Up track 3 miles west of Banff - 3 times, fighting fire and fixing pump at garage and took to fire, smashed crank case and piston arm on chain driver unit, unable to get pump to work satisfactorily, up to fire after supper with Warren and Mumford, out to buffalo pasture and Bankhead Station, heard of fire in elk pasture, phoned Phillips of fire near Baker Creek, message from Stinson, no steps taken to protect other stacks if fire gets away, 12 hours, 8 or 9 miles speeder and auto.

October 7th - Fine forenoon, cloudy afternoon, snow at night

At fire 1 mile west of Banff all day, fire broke out again near starting point, Warren managed to get it under, 10 hours, pump worked okay today, 8 miles speeder and auto.

October 9th - Cloudy, cold

To meadows, caught horse and killed for Zoo in afternoon with Wood, took supplies to Castle for Stinson and Mumford, to town, 8 miles rode, 47 miles car.

October 15th - Fine

To Castle Mountain with supplies etc. for Mumford, 2 bags, cut open bear that died in Zoo and took to Garbage Grounds, found him to have very bad teeth and also large piece of meat stuck in throat, to Bankhead with load of supplies for Warren to take to Red Deer, 98 miles auto.

October 17th - Fine

Killed horse for Zoo (Bert Ward's) at sawmill, helped load it on dray in afternoon, then took field horses to pasture west of Banff, then on to Mount Edith Pass, 4 hours misc., 4 hours patrol, 12 miles rode.

October 19th - Fine

West on Auto Road to Sawback hill with Warden Wood, looking for car reported by McAulay, 7:30 back at 9:00 p.m., out again at 10 p.m. on Auto Road till 7:30 a.m., watching Amoss and Joe Blair - suspected of killing game, met Amoss at 2:00 a.m. walking towards town, he immediately jumped for bush when he saw us, went through his car earlier in the evening (nothing doing), waiting around gate - 2 hours, 36 miles auto and walked.

October 20th - Fine

Came in off Auto Road at 7:30, had breakfast, then up to Chief's office, rode west in afternoon, found carcass of young ram (spring lamb) at point near sulphur spring where we searched Amoss' car last evening, came to town, reported to Supt., took Wood to see sheep, searched Amoss' car again near entrance to Auto Road, then went and brought carcass to town, 8 miles saddle horse, 22 miles auto, 10 hours patrol.

October 21st - Fine

To Observatory with Supt. and Gov. General's party - 6 horses, saw Wood skin sheep and found it had been shot with 22 bullet, 16 miles rode and walked.

October 22nd - Cold, stormy

Up to office making report for Supt. on game case, west on Auto Road to Sawback hill, on hill looking for possible evidence with Warren, 16 miles walked.

October 27th - Fair

West to meadows with horses in forenoon, west on Auto Road to Massive, took Wood to cabin and patrolling road, 31 miles horse and auto, saw McLeod, came to house at 6:30 to get rifle sealed, 6 mm, said J. Brewster wanted it sealed.

October 28th - Fair

Killed horse for Zoo (government pack horse no. 44), helped man load meat, took boys to Rodd and down to feed beavers, 8 or 9 miles auto and rode.

October 30th - Fine

Spray River to White Man Pass with hay for Spray, 28 miles rode.

October 31st - Fine

West to pasture, rounded up horses and took to yard, branded all on hoof, then took to lower Buffalo Park, also took Heinie (sorrel pony from overseas), to sheep pasture, Hot Springs, Cave and Basin, 28 miles car and saddle horse.

November 1919

November 3rd - Fine

To Bankhead, Buffalo Park with packs for Warren and Wright, helped them pack to go to Red Deer, up to Chief's office and west along Auto Road - 2nd Lake, 18 miles car.

November 5th - Fine

About town forenoon, west on Auto Road to 7 mile board with Chief Warden and Deputy Wood, looking for large head for Chief to take pictures, to falls and at stable, black car went out of commission and I could not start it, got towed home by McAulay, 18 miles auto.

November 11th - Cold, clear, windy

To feed beaver, patrolling Auto Road and following man's tracks up on hill near 6 mile sand hill, night patrol - 2 hours, 18 miles auto.

November 18th - Fine

West to Sawback forenoon, shipped elk horns to James at Jasper Park, west on Auto Road to Johnston Canyon with Chief Warden, 42 miles auto.

November 20th - Cloudy, windy

To Buffalo Park and inspected mountain sheep ram that was found dead, found beast had broken neck, cut off head, meat was no good, apparently been dead some days, also skinned elk that had been killed by train going west, cut up meat for Zoo, west on Auto Road to Sawback, 25 miles auto no. 4.

November 23rd - Rain

To Buffalo Park, Cave Avenue, beaver enclosure, Auto

Road to 6 mile sand hill and station, took vet to park to see bull yak and to Zoo to see polar bear, 20 miles auto.

November 29th - Cold

Auto Road west to Massive, took stores up for Wood, then to Buffalo Park and skinned bull yak that had been inspected by vet on Sunday, Nov. 23rd, found large abscess on top of head, finished skinning after dark, 30 miles auto no. 3.

December 1919

December 3rd - Warmer

Up on Squaw Mountain, found where fawn deer had been killed and dragged, apparently large lynx, Sundance Canyon Road, 12 miles rode.

December 4th - Fine

West on Auto Road, at 6 mile sand hill saw large ram - old - up on side hill, upon going up to look him over, found he had something the matter with his lower jaw, so I shot him at once and found he had his nose and lower jaw smashed, I took his insides out and came to town for car, then brought carcass to town and skinned out same, head had 42 inch curve and about 16 inch base, also saw several fine specimens (getting dark), 24 miles saddle horse and auto.

December 5th - Cold

To office forenoon then east to Canmore and Gap and Kananaskis, took lumber to Canmore, got pack outfit from Kananaskis and sheep meat and head from Gap - shot by Latam, 56 miles auto.

December 9th - Very cold

Down to beaver enclosure and sized up layout, found creek not yet flooded and water running over dam, reported same to Chief at office, 3 or 4 miles walked.

December 10th - Cold, 40 below

Not out.

December 12th - Cold

Across in woods north of railway yards and moose pasture, following tracks around moose pasture, but found nothing suspicious, got report that Amoss had gone to end of

Squirrel Street in car then gone down the track, 4 or 5 miles walked.

December 13th - Milder

Along moose pasture fence to Forty Mile Crossing forenoon and through moose pasture and back to sheep pasture with Warren looking for possible poachers, tracks re: Amoss - he was down the track the day before, 10 miles walked.

December 19th - Mild

To beaver enclosure and cut hole in ice near dam, got chain repaired to fasten gate, took nuts and corn down in afternoon and left near hole in ice for beaver, west on Auto Road to Mount Edith Pass trail, washed out crank case of auto with coal oil, 15 miles auto.

December 20th - Mild

Banff to Kananaskis with Warren, west on Auto Road to sucker spring, 61 miles auto, saw Warden Latam near Canmore.

December 21st - Mild

Along moose fence to Tote Road and Squaw Mountain, west on Auto Road to seven mile spring, met Supt. J. McCowan, Hugh Gordon, 18 miles auto and walked.

December 24th - Snow and rain all day

About town, to Cave and Basin, Sundance Road, took typewriter from Dignall's house to Supt., Buffalo Park and beaver enclosure, 15 miles auto and walked.

December 27th - Cloudy

East on Auto Road to Kananaskis, helped move shack across road, took Griffiths from Canmore to gateway, home 6:30, 56 miles auto.

Walter and Rosabelle Peyto's children (Left to right) - Walter, Harold, Edith, Syd, Stan.

View of Mount Rundle from 3rd Lake. Whyte Museum of the Canadian Rockies. V263 NA71-4527.

C. Phillips and H. Sibbald with first fire truck - 1920. Whyte
Museum of the Canadian Rockies. V573 NA66-2178.

Nineteen Twenty

January 1920
January 10th - Fine
Moose pasture to Tote Road and along Squaw Mountain to log chute and Auto Road, home by station, east to Canmore with Warren to see S. Stirton, 37 miles auto and walked.
January 13th - Chinook
Along moose fence to Tote Road, across Forty Mile to sheep pasture, through Buffalo Park, home by Bankhead Road, west on Auto Road to Mount Edith Pass, moved sheep head in pasture, measured same, 17 inches base, 39 inches curve, 14 miles rode and walked.
January 14th - Cloudy and snow
West to 2nd Lake and meadows, to Bankhead Lodge with Warren and Cyril Childe, to lower Loop and east to 7 mile creek, 40 miles by saddle horse and car.
January 17th - Snowed heavy all day
About town forenoon, 3 miles walked, received parcel of 5 foot snowshoes from Government, larger mesh, not much good.
January 22nd - Cold, 40 below
About town and to Chief's office, getting line up on when he would arrive with elk, 3 miles walked.
January 23rd - Cold
Banff to Duthil and return, speeder and train, unloading elk Duthil and Banff - 12 hours, getting young elk in stable.
January 24th - Cold
At stables skinning out elk for Zoo, sent meat to Zoo, and loading young live elk in box stall - 8 hours, 4 or 5 miles walked, borrowed 1 length of stove pipe and elbow from Moffatt's house for Wood.

February 1920
February 3rd - Fine
To stable tending elk - 2 hours, down around station and to Chief's office making up car report, Upper Anthracite Road

to old rifle range, crossed river to Loop and home by falls, out with Sanson looking for specimen of mule deer, ran into yearling female, shot it and found her leg to have been broken in two places, Sanson wants same for specimen, 10 miles walking and snowshoeing.

February 4th - Fine

Moose pasture fence to Tote Road and Squaw Mountain and to Chief's office, to Loop and Golf Links looking for large buck with Warren - out till 7 p.m., 12 miles riding and snowshoeing.

February 8th - Fine, Sunday

West along moose fence to Tote Road and followed ski tracks through woods looking for place where trap had been set as the ski tracks led from place where one of my traps had been stolen, no luck, 4 or 5 miles snowshoeing, caught lynx.

February 11th - Fine

Up Squaw Mountain to head of chute with lunch for snowshoeing party, including Supt. Wardle and wife, made fire and boiled water, 6 miles rode.

February 13th - Fine

To ski jump and Buffalo Park with Chief Warden etc. to see jumps, about town, 6 miles auto and walked.

February 14th - Fine

West on Auto Road to sucker spring and Sundance and Healy Trail, about town forenoon, ran in the ski-joring races, 15 miles rode.

February 17th - Fine

About town forenoon, to Holmes' funeral in afternoon, to station, shipped speeder to Lake Louise and returned two from Castle and put in car shed, 4 or 5 miles walked.

February 19th - Snow all day

Healy Lodge to Banff, too wet to work forenoon, at station in afternoon fixing up team and looking after elk, got door for Healy, hauled some lumber for my own house, 8 miles drove and walked.

February 26th - Cloudy, warm
About town in afternoon, home forenoon - wife not feeling well.
February 27th to March 2nd - Fine
Sick.

March 1920
March 5th to 11th
Sick, cold, neuralgia.
March 12th - Mild
About town and Chief's office, to Bankhead Station and dressed horse for Zoo (Brewster's), 10 miles car and walked.
March 25th - Mild
Up to Chief's office forenoon, and hung up hides to dry, took 2 elk from stables to Buffalo Park and turned out, 7 or 8 miles walked and drove.
March 30th - Stormy
Cave Avenue to Sundance Canyon and Healy Trails, to Golf Links and rock crusher, picked up Mr. Rat, walked down to beaver enclosure, saw tracks, first since big freeze up, 12 miles drove.

April 1920
April 1st - Stormy
To Chief's office in forenoon and about town, Buffalo Park, to sheep pasture with McAulay and Cave Avenue, 8 miles drove.
April 2nd - Cold, 8 below, Good Friday
About town hunting for deer with broken leg in afternoon, 4 or 5 miles walked.
April 3rd - Cold, zero
Hunting for deer with broken leg north of station - found him, Cave Avenue and Spray Avenue, Buffalo Park road, 10 miles walked and drove.
April 12th - Mild
Spray Valley to old logging road with Rodd from Fish

Hatchery and with men and outfit going to Spray Lakes, to beaver enclosure and to Chief's office, fed beaver, snow very deep up Spray Valley, 18 miles rode and drove.

April 26th - Fine

Sundance and Healy Trail to Healy Lodge, crossed river, home on Auto Road, took boat up river and tested out telephone, 14 miles rode.

April 27th - Fair

Cave Avenue and station, west on Auto Road to Second Lake and sucker spring with movie artists, Hot Springs in afternoon, took Chief Warden and Supt.'s baggage to station.

April 30th - Stormy

Banff to Kananaskis and return, took Rodd to Canmore and Curren to Gap, 56 miles auto.

May 1920

May 1st - Stormy

Bankhead Station and dairy, across Cascade River to point where mountain lion had been seen by George Harrison, riding around over hills looking for possible chance of shooting lion, back again in afternoon, set traps around carcass, 15 miles rode.

May 2nd - Fair

To top of Anthracite hill, waded river to traps, no luck, also put poplar trees in for beavers, 18 miles auto and walked.

May 7th - Fine, warm

West to Sawback to 3 miles, to Loop and two trips to 5 mile board, 5 fires set by engine on no. 4 passenger train, turned out extra gang, fire in dead rotten timber, grass and willow, 35 miles auto.

May 8th - Fine

West to Sawback hill, put out salt for sheep, looked over fires etc., got packs from hatchery, to stable, arranged for Latam and Wright to go to Spray Lakes, also for Griffiths to go to Calgary with me for horses (to Calgary at night), 98 miles auto and train.

May 9th - Cloudy
Calgary Stockyards to Cochrane, 25 miles rode.
May 10th - Stormy
Cochrane to Kananaskis, 35 miles rode.
May 11th - Showery
Kananaskis to Banff, branded all horses and put in pasture, 30 miles rode.
May 16th - Fine
To CPR stables, found deer yearling lying a little off the road where it had been hit by an automobile. I killed this animal and took carcass to the Zoo ice house, fed horses in pasture, 5 miles auto.
May 17th - Rain, wind
Banff to Castle with stores and Brooks, and to get outfit and leave him at Massive, car 40 miles.
May 18th - Fair
Cave Avenue, took HES to station, to Buffalo Park, put two yak in corrals, helped Curren catch horses, Loop and Golf Links, car 15 miles.
May 20th - Fine
Taking horses to Castle, moving wire - 8 miles west of Castle, installed phone at Chateau at Johnston Creek, 40 miles auto.
May 26th - Fine
To horse pasture, helped catch horses and worked on corral, getting out freight, loading yak at park and taking to station and also loading on train at night, 12 hours misc., 25 miles car.
May 27th - Stormy, rain
Taking freight to station for Lake Louise, to horse pasture and beaver enclosure, at Crown yard taking out stalls and floor - making store room for game wardens' outfits, 10 miles car, Garrett reported black bear at Hot Springs.
May 29th - Stormy
West to Massive, horse pasture and beaver enclosure, west to sucker spring catching fish for polar bear, 35 miles auto.

May 30th - Stormy (Sunday)

To Hot Springs, set trap for bear in afternoon, to Hot Springs in evening, took bear out of trap and hung up, shot by Curren, 10 miles auto.

June 1920

June 2nd - Cloudy

Banff to Canmore and to Deadman's Cabin on south side with supplies and men to work with Warden Curren, 45 miles auto.

June 4th - Fine

About town forenoon, west to Castle Mountain and Massive, took grub, hoe and oiler to Mumford, hauled hay from track to Massive Lodge, helped Wood pull 2 quills out of dog, 45 miles auto.

June 8th - Stormy

Took Mr. Wardle and Stewart to Cave and Basin, got phone call from Griffiths that horses had arrived, notified Chief who took Latam to go for them, west on Auto Road to 7 mile spring and to Loop, 26 miles auto.

June 9th - Fine

Banff to Canmore Lodge for horses, helped Latam bring same to Banff and branded them and put in pasture, 30 miles saddle horse.

June 10th - Fine

Took Chief Warden to station, west on Auto Road to sucker spring, saw pile of garbage, examined with Fyfe, found who had dumped it, had it removed, Fyfe measured green timber, killed wild horse for Zoo, to Carrot Creek with truck driver for McAulay, to Exshaw with gasoline etc. for red trucks, got stuck - home 7 p.m., 70 miles auto.

June 11th - Showery

Took express to station (tires and battery from red cars that came from Calgary), to office, took pack outfit to Bankhead, to Minnewanka for Wright's grub, repaired line on road, took express to station for Fox, 29 miles auto.

June 13th - Fine

West on Auto Road to Johnston Canyon, looked for cougar on Auto Road and Tunnel Mountain, Phillips had car, 35 miles auto and walked.

June 14th - Hot

Banff to Kananaskis and west to seven mile spring in evening by 8 mile board with Edwards looking at washout, 72 miles auto.

June 15th - Hot

Took Sanson to Lake Minnewanka, at pasture and lower Buffalo Park catching horses and moving Walcott bunch, got horses shod and moved outfit from stores to wardens' storeroom, 30 miles auto and saddle horse.

June 16th - Fine, hot

To horse pasture and Chief's office, west on Auto Road in evening to Sawback, met Warden Wood and wife at 7 mile spring, to Spray River, took horses to blacksmith, waited to get stores for Griffiths, 20 miles auto and saddle horse.

June 17th - Hot

To Canmore with grub and outfit for Griffiths and rake for Latam, straightened up fire outfit - 2 hours, west on Auto Road to Massive with Tex Wood's grub, met Warden Phillips at Mount Edith going west - 8 hours patrol, 56 miles auto.

June 18th - Fine

West to Massive with Sanson forenoon, west to Castle Mountain and old internment camp, got latrine from camp for Johnston Canyon, brought Mumford to town - sick, 70 miles auto, saw 10 lambs in one bunch, 5 large rams at sucker spring, saw black bear at salt lick - sulphur spring.

June 24th - Showery

Cave Avenue, Sundance Canyon and Healy Trail, repaired telephone - 1 hour, 3 hours patrol, west on Auto Road to Castle, brought latrine to Johnston Canyon and put up for use of public - 5 hours, 48 miles car.

June 27th - Fine

Followed Whiskey Creek and Forty Mile Creek through

pastures, looked for illegal fishermen, 5 miles walked.

June 29th

At station, yard, about town, to Canmore Lodge in afternoon, helped Warren pack up for Spray, fixed up Supt.'s horse, took outfit for Latam to Canmore with Chief Warden, 5 hours misc., 5 hours patrol, 30 miles auto.

June 30th - Fine

Put tank on fire pumps and tried out pump at river, west on Auto Road to Castle and then to Boom Creek, Vermilion Summit and Boundary Cabin - 5 hours patrol, 66 miles auto, pumped water off Auto Road in two places.

July 1920

July 1st - Fine

Sundance Canyon and Golf Links, along Whiskey Creek and Forty Mile Creek - watching kids fishing, 25 miles auto and walked.

July 2nd - Fine

To Chief's office and gathered up stores, east to Canmore Lodge with supplies for Curren, west to Massive Lodge with supplies for Wood, 52 miles auto.

July 5th - Showery

At stable waiting for papers to ship horses, at garage - fixed car and pump, rushed to Buffalo Park, found Woodworth dead in field, having fallen from his horse, broke his neck, to Banff for H.E. Sibbald, to park and took charge of animals, 18 miles auto.

The Banff Crag & Canyon - July 10th, 1920

Passing of an Old Timer

A deeply regrettable accident occurred Monday afternoon when Ben Woodworth, caretaker of the Buffalo Park, fell from his horse and sustained a broken neck. He was engaged in his daily occupation of rounding up the buffalo herd on horseback when he fell backward from his saddle, presumably from a sudden attack of heart failure.

The only witness of the accident was Robert Bennett, a chauffeur in the employ of the Brewster Transport Co. who had driven a carload of tourists into the animal enclosure.

When he saw that Mr. Woodworth did not rise from the ground he hastened to his assistance, but was too late to render aid as the unfortunate man was already past human help. Bennett notified the family and later on phoned the government office.

An inquest was held Monday night and a verdict was rendered that "deceased came to his death accidentally while in the discharge of his duties."

The funeral was held Thursday afternoon from the family residence to the Banff cemetery. Dr. White of Canmore took charge of the service, while undertaker Reid looked after the arrangements. The funeral cortege was a long one, testifying to the regard in which deceased was held by all classes of the community.

July 6th to 8th - Fine
At Buffalo Park all day.
July 10th - Hot
Banff to Castle and scene of fire, Castle to Johnston Canyon and back to Castle, loaded up pump etc., and helped Mumford put up camp at canyon, 29 miles auto, to Buffalo Park with oats in evening.
July 15th - Hot
To lower Buffalo Park, caught horse and got shod for Rodd, Loop and Sundance Canyon, CPR Hotel, Hot Springs, Cave and Basin and Auto Road, put out coal oil with Sanson for mosquitoes, 32 miles auto and saddle horse.
July 17th - Hot
To lower Buffalo Park, caught horses, to sheep pasture and got Russian pony and put in corral at Museum, turned out saddle horse, 10 miles rode.
July 18th - Hot
East to Kananaskis and Park line and return, took Walker to Cochrane, 64 miles auto, saw several sheep on road 2 miles west of Exshaw.
July 20th - Hot, showery at night
To stable and yard, got out shovels for fire fighting, moved fire warden to Camp Ground and got outfit out for Warden Naylor to go to Vermilion Summit, 10 miles auto.

July 21st - Hot, thunderstorm evening

West on Auto Road to Castle and south on Banff-Windermere Road to Vermilion Summit and then to Tokumm Creek, took outfit for Warden Naylor to eastern boundary of Kootenay Park, took Chief to Castle, Mumford at Johnston Creek, 75 miles auto no. 2.

July 22nd - Showery forenoon, fine afternoon

Putting up fire notices around outskirts of town, Buffalo Park, Cave Avenue, falls, out with Sanson putting out coal oil - afternoon, Recreation Grounds, to fire wardens' camp at falls after supper with bed, full of hay, tent in dirty condition, 15 miles auto.

July 24th - Fine

Office, to station with express for Canmore, out with Sanson with coal oil, to Hot Springs with tobacco for men on trail, fixed wheel on no. 2 car, took gasoline to Wright - Lake Minnewanka, 25 miles car.

July 29th - Fine, thunder at night

Cave and Basin, Hot Springs with Mr. Stewart, west on Auto Road evening to Sawback hill, got pack horse shod and turned horse in field, 10 miles auto, got Mr. Harkin to wire for pumps, hose etc.

July 31st - Fine

To office, west on Auto Road to Sawback, to Buffalo Park, about town and packing and shipping supplies to Lake Louise on midnight train for fire fighters, sealed guns for Mr. Curtiss, got call from Phillips at 6 p.m. to send grub, saw Warren who went to Lake Louise, was told by Warren that Supt. satisfied by the way I had run things, everything OK.

August 1920

August 1st - Fair

To camp on Auto Road, to station for parcel (Supt.'s order), took eyelets to Garrett, got call to Lake Minnewanka, notified Supt. to send Nichol and 7 men to lake, unable to leave town, out after supplies, sent pump and grub for men, Standly took charge of pump, fire under control, 42 miles auto.

August 2nd - Fine

To lake for fire fighters, and to Canmore with grub for Griffiths and about town, 45 miles auto, 13 hours.

August 3rd

Loop to Camp Grounds and Police Camp, to Camp Grounds, Spray Avenue and Sundance Canyon, station and Golf Links at night, about town looking for car owner of what was left of fire west of Cave and Basin, fire at cold spring ½ mile west of Cave and Basin - camp fire left, one at end of Canyon Road - picnic fire - 4 square feet, saw owner of car and notified him he would be summoned for breach of regulations, also warned him not to leave town, 30 miles auto.

August 4th - Fine

At office and police barracks, laid information against T.W. Lodge for leaving fire on Canyon Road - 2 square feet, at garage oiling up and overhauling etc. fire auto, at court - witness against T.W. Lodge, fined $5.00 and costs, out to fire on Tunnel Mountain (St. Julien) townsite, called out police car loaded with police, two men at fire all night, left men at fire at 12:30, 17 hours, 20 miles auto.

August 5th - Fine

To fire and brought men to camp for breakfast - 8:30, took out two others, got hose from Golf Links, worked on fire all day, took hose back to Links, went and looked around scene of fire after supper - 13 hours, 15 miles auto.

August 7th - Fine

Sundance Canyon moving fire wardens, to Buffalo Park helping move sheep, then to Loop and turned them loose, to horse pasture, caught up horse for Commissioner's use, west to road camp with men, put saddle horse in stable, broke loose at night, 23 miles auto.

August 8th - Fine

West to Castle and south on Windermere Road to summit cabin with supplies for Warden Naylor, took fire warning notice to Johnston Canyon, 64 miles auto.

August 11th - Fine

Sundance Canyon, Loop to police camp, fixed phone, west on Auto Road to 7 mile board, took drills etc. for Healy Creek Trail gang, about town, found fire in two spots - apparently cigarettes - 2 square feet, 30 miles auto.

August 12th - Fine

To station and got crate of Canada Geese, put same in Zoo, Cave Avenue and Sundance Canyon, Loop and Camp Ground, Loop at night to see if sheep were down on flat, put up fire notices around engineers' camp.

August 14th - Warm, very smoky

To pasture, helped Warren catch horses, helped him pack up to go to Kananaskis Lakes fire, station, Hot Springs with eyelets, Sundance Canyon, found small fire burning, 5 square feet, about town, expecting call any minute, 20 miles auto.

August 15th - Hot, smoky dull afternoon, windy at night

Sundance Canyon, about town, station, Auto Road, fire left at picnic ground - 3 square feet, 20 miles auto, 9:30 - Chief rang up to say he had heard from Wood that fire had burnt head of Bryant Creek, Wood could not get through to fire fighters who have only one way to get out via Simpson River or crossing, hemmed in.

August 18th - Cloudy

To Healy Lodge via Sundance Road, tried to fix phone at cabin, east to Canmore to help Latam fight fire - home 11:45 p.m., 34 miles auto, 14 miles saddle horse, first airplane from Morley Station (Chiniki Creek) came to Banff and circled over town.

August 19th - Cloudy and warmer

To Sundance Canyon, ordered men to move camp, to Canmore helping Latam put out fire all day, fire in centre burning coal outcrop, reported this to manager of Canmore Coal Co., 45 miles auto, 3 hours patrol, 6 hours fire.

August 21st - Warm, windy

To Banff and returned to Castle and to Banff at night, then

back to Castle and back to Banff, fighting fire in between, 112 miles auto, fire on Tunnel Mountain - 40 square feet, NBS reported, about 15 trees, 5 foot scrub.

The Banff Crag & Canyon - August 21st, 1920
Fire Guards Needed

A dense pall of smoke overhung the village the first of this week, especially heavy Tuesday morning and many rumours were current of approaching disaster which might endanger the village.

Forest fires were reported as raging at Mount Assiniboine, the head of the Kananaskis Lakes, at Simpson Pass and at the Spray Lakes. One of the Alpine Club camps was in the path of the approaching flames, but the camp and effects were moved several miles and escaped unharmed.

While the village of Banff was in no immediate danger, still it but emphasizes the fact that no proper fire guards are placed to guard against a near approach of forest fires. This warning should be sufficient to have such fire guards prepared at once.

Over twelve years ago Crag and Canyon persistently advocated fire guards for the village and at length some attention was given to this matter. But the fire guards have not been kept in repair and in many instances are at the present time covered with a growth of young timber and almost obliterated.

A forest fire, fanned by a strong wind like that of Monday night, once started on Sulphur Mountain and it's "goodbye" Banff. Not all the government equipment nor government men - provided they all turned out - would be able to check the flames.

August 22nd - Fine

To Castle Mountain with Chief Warden, started pump and left Warden Naylor in charge, 40 miles auto.

August 25th - Cloudy, some rain at night

West on Auto Road to Castle, south to Vermilion Summit with supplies for Warden Naylor, gathered up hose and pump etc. and brought to town, to Lake Minnewanka with gasoline for Warden Wright, to Chief's office, 72 miles auto.

September 1920
September 2nd - Fine
To police camp at night - to have 10 men ready to go fight fire on Summit, Auto Road west to Sawback, Sundance Canyon, 18 miles auto.
September 3rd - Fine
To Buffalo Park, caught up saddle horse and got shod, caught up horse for Supt., hauled freight to station for Phillips, took oats to Sundance for police horses on summit, 18 miles auto.
September 5th - Fine, clouded up - evening
Sundance Canyon and Healy Trail to Brewster and Douglas Creeks with Chief Warden, looking for possible fire guard, 26 miles rode, Wood came in with police and said the fire had got beyond control.
September 6th - Labour Day, showery, very heavy rain storm last night
Took hay to Wood (Tex), got horses from pasture for Supt. and Wardle, got Chief's horse shod, 7 or 8 miles car and horse.
September 7th - Fine
To pasture and caught horse, took horse to lower Buffalo Park and butchered for Zoo - 3 hours, took hay to Bill Peyto - feed for horse, gathered up government outfit for Supt. and Chief Warden and highway engineers' trip to Kootenay, 10 miles auto and saddle horse.
September 8th - Fine
To pasture, caught horses, about town, gathered up outfit for Warren, T. Wood and myself, to Healy and Brewster Creeks to mouth of Douglas Creek and return, left Wood at logging camp, saw smoke rising over ridge, came to town at dark, left word at police camp for 20 men in morning to cut trail into scene of fire at head of Douglas Creek, unable to get Major Douglas on phone so I was carrying out Chief Warden's orders regarding taking men out, 28 miles rode.

September 9th - Cloudy

Took tools to Sundance Road for police, to Alpine Club to get Rink and Fitten to pack in grub to Douglas Creek, took grub to Healy Creek in car, asked them to bring back my pack horse, 20 miles auto, took freight to station etc.

September 11th - Cloudy

Douglas Creek to Banff, about town, through moose pasture to Forty Mile crossing, cut fence open per Chief's orders to let moose out, got outfit of grub ready for police at Douglas Creek, 20 miles saddle horse and auto, Police Sergeant McCarthy came in and reported fire still burning.

September 13th - Cloudy, rain forenoon

To office forenoon, gathered up outfit for Massive, took same to Massive Lodge and Mumford to Johnston Canyon, tried out phone at canyon, brought Mrs. Orr to town, 35 miles auto.

September 14th - Cloudy

To horse pasture, got horses and saddle for Bill Peyto, to Golf Links about horns that were stolen, fixed spring on fire auto and got ready for trip to Vermilion camp, 12 miles auto.

September 16th - Showery

West on Auto Road to Castle and south to Vermilion River road camp and warden's cabin on Moose Creek Trail, to Marble Canyon and to road camp, saw Chief Warden and Supt. Malcolm Annon, Joe Blair, Melvin, also Warden Naylor, stayed with Naylor overnight, 45 miles auto and saddle horse.

September 17th - Fine

Vermilion Cabin to road camp and ochre beds, got shoe put on Wardle's horse, then brought Chief's horse to Massive, got to Banff in car, 35 miles saddle horse and car.

September 18th - Rain forenoon, fine afternoon

Sundance Canyon, tried out telephone to Mather's Boathouse and Recreation Grounds, killed old horse for Mather, west on Auto Road to Massive Lodge, took Wood out to bring Chief Warden and Supt.'s horses to town, also checked up tools etc. left by Tex Wood, 32 miles auto.

September 20th - Showery

To fire at 1:30 a.m. - Beattie Block, west on Auto Road to big meadow with Warden Wood, brought horses to town and impounded same, went west to 6 mile sand hill, moose killed on track, helped skin and took to Zoo, 18 miles auto and saddle horse.

September 23rd - Cloudy, cool

Changing coyotes and foxes at Zoo, shipping outfit to Kootenay in afternoon, 8 hours misc., 7 or 8 hours auto.

September 26th - Cloudy, windy

West on Auto Road to 5 mile board looking for car supposed to have been left by poachers, accompanied by Assistant Supt., found car to belong to Quigley, waited until party came off mountain, nothing doing, 20 miles auto.

October 1920

October 1st - Rain

West on Auto Road to Johnston Canyon, Castle Mountain to canyon and returned to Castle Mountain, moved Mumford camp to house at Castle, set traps for rats in house, brought outfit for Warden Wood to Banff, met Warden Naylor from Kootenay Park at Castle - he gave me an order for stores, brought Mumford to Banff, cut off telephone at canyon, took hay to corrals, 46 miles auto.

October 4th - Showery

To corral and fed horses, to office, took Chief to station, to Golf Links with salt for sheep, east to Canmore Lodge with feed for Latam, 35 miles auto.

October 6th - Fine

West to Castle, south on Vermilion Road to Vermilion Cabin with supplies for Warden Naylor, got telephone message from Mrs. Staple that saddle horse had been killed on track during night, reported same to Mr. Wood, Assistant Supt., 79 miles auto, told Naylor to go to Kootenay Crossing and meet Alworth.

October 8th - Cloudy

To Loop and Golf Links, moved telephone line along new road - 3 hours, west to Sawback west switch with C.W. Moffatt, killed bull that had been hit by train, 20 miles auto.

October 9th - Cloudy, cool

To garage, repaired auto no. 3 - got ready for Warren, took general utility car and drove men for water line to Loop camp, west on Auto Road to Castle and picked up teamster for Mr. Wardle and took him south on Vermilion Road and caught tote team at Marble Canyon, saw Mumford, 68 miles auto (spare).

October 12th - Stormy

Up Spray to Loop, loaded up 4 goats with Bill Peyto, took same to park and turned loose, met Supt. at station - 11 p.m., 20 miles drove.

October 13th - Fine

To Castle with supplies for Mumford, brought back part of Chief's outfit, to park after saddle and took to station for Supt., took Fyfe to Minnewanka sawmill, 56 miles auto.

October 14th - Stormy

Helped Curren pack, took Fyfe and blacksmith to Kananaskis and hauled hay for horses, 56 miles auto.

October 15th - Cold, snow

To office, Cave Avenue, to station with HES, met Naylor, took battery out of fire car to be charged, hauled up meat from Moffatt's and took to Zoo, 575 lbs., 10 miles auto.

October 16th - Fine

To office and station forenoon, about town, to field and fed horses, gathered up horses in afternoon and took to upper meadows, caught up "Goldie," my saddle horse, 10 miles saddle horse.

October 19th - Fine

Cave Avenue, Fish Hatchery, to pasture and fed horses, getting out supplies etc. and packing and shipping same to Caine - Red Deer, to Buffalo Park with Chief Warden and Supt., 10 miles auto.

October 20th - Fine

To office, to field and fed horse, to Castle and Vermilion Cabin, with Mr. McDonald of B.C. Forestry Dept., checked up tools belonging to F. Dept., 76 miles auto, home 7 p.m.

October 22nd - fine

To field and fed horses, to station looking for pheasants from Vancouver, repaired car, to Buffalo Park with wire for fence, helped cut goats' feet, got wire for Sanson and Fyfe to make trap to catch swan, took same to 2nd Lake, 15 miles auto.

October 23rd - Fine

To Buffalo Park, station, Auto Road, west to Third Lake, looking for swans, were four - now gone, east to Canmore Lodge with supplies for Curren, to field and fed horses, 40 miles auto.

November 1920

November 1st - Fine

To Buffalo Park looking at cow buffalo, around town, office and Zoo, shipped outfit for Forestry B.C., took buffalo crate out of car at Zoo with Mr. Wood and Edwards, 10 miles walked and rode.

November 3rd - Cloudy

To Castle with supplies and hauled wire up Vermilion Road with Warden Naylor, 70 miles auto.

November 5th - Fine

At stores and wardens' storeroom, Cave and Basin, moved stores etc. to wardens' storeroom, at garage in afternoon, put radiator in car, hauled badger from station to Zoo, 5 miles car.

November 9th

West on Auto Road to Castle and north to Black's camp with Warden Naylor and Mr. Wardle, helped Naylor start car at road camp and brought same to Castle, 67 miles auto.

November 11th - Fine

Gathered up supplies and telephone material for Gap-Kananaskis line and took same to Deadman's Cabin, 42 miles auto, met Warden Latam at Canmore and Curren at Gap.

November 12th - Fine

At Chief's office forenoon - fixing up report and diary, west to Castle Mountain with mechanic to look over car belonging to Wardle's camp, found car in bad shape, needs overhauling and new carburetor, 45 miles auto.

November 16th - Stormy (snow)

Castle to Vermilion Summit with Watrick and camp outfit, then took two loads of wire to summit, 72 miles auto.

November 18th - Stormy

West on Auto Road to Temple and Lake Louise with wire, 108 miles auto, saw Warden Phillips at Lake Louise.

November 19th - Fine

Castle to Banff with Warden Naylor who brought red truck to town, repaired Banff-Canmore line near falls, 25 miles auto, shot dog of A.N. Saddington.

November 23rd - Fine

To upper meadows and brought in horses in forenoon, killed one for Zoo, took rest to horse pastures and went to station with Warren and got female deer that was brought in by train crew from Duthil, 10 miles saddle horse.

December 1920

December 1st - Cloudy

West on Auto Road to Castle Mountain with Warden Naylor, repaired phone and made up new phone for summit, 40 miles auto.

December 3rd - Fine

Gathered up supplies and took same to Warden Curren at Gap, home 10 p.m., met Warden Latam at Canmore Lodge, 43 miles auto.

December 8th - Fine, cold

West on Auto Road to 10 mile board with wire for phone, east on Auto Road to Canmore Lodge for Curren's outfit from Kananaskis River, 44 miles auto.

December 18th - East wind

West on Auto Road to 4 mile board with wire gang, east on Auto Road to Kananaskis and Morley Station, inspecting forestry telephone to see how buzzer worked and got name of buzzer, 98 miles auto.

December 22nd - Cold, 23 below

West on Auto Road to 5 mile board forenoon and afternoon, took Warren and men to work and brought them home, helped catch monkeys at Zoo, helped Warren cut posts and hauled same, 22 miles auto.

December 27th - Cloudy, warmer

West on Auto Road to 4 mile board, Golf Links and Loop, west on Auto Road to Massive Lodge, brought line gang to town, took Warden Naylor home, 36 miles auto.

December 28th - Fair

West to 5 mile board, loaded up supplies for Massive, then to Massive and Castle, worked 1 hour on telephone with Warren, 50 miles auto.

Walter Peyto.

Scotty Wright in patrol boat at Lake Minnewanka - 1920. Whyte
Museum of the Canadian Rockies. V573 NA66-2182.

Tex Wood children at Massive Cabin. Whyte Museum of the
Canadian Rockies. V573 NA66-1646.

Nineteen Twenty One

January 1921
January 1st - Cloudy, warm
West on Auto Road to Massive Lodge, brought in Watrick and outfit, 24 miles auto.
January 2nd - Snow
Up town and got deer from Dr. Learn's residence, spring buck, took to Zoo, 3 miles auto.
January 4th - Cloudy
Buffalo Park, west on Auto Road to Massive Lodge with Chief Warden, took supplies to Warden Brown, brought back sleighs for Wilkins, road very heavy, brought in post hole tools from 6 mile sand hill, home 7 p.m., heavy snow at night.
January 5th - Cloudy
To office forenoon and fixed up engineer's car, east on Auto Road to Carrot Creek with McAulay and Chief Warden breaking trail, 20 miles auto no. 5.
January 10th - Fine
Auto Road and Squaw Mountain in forenoon, east to Canmore with Fyfe on inspection trip in afternoon, car 6 (engineer's), 35 miles auto and walked.
January 24th - Fine
To lower Buffalo Park, went with caretaker to see buffalo bull, could not get him up, found where they had been fighting, went to office and reported condition of animal to Chief, went to park in afternoon and killed bull and dressed meat for Zoo, brought head and hide to town, 10 miles rode.
January 27th - Cloudy
Auto Road west to 1st Lake, Cave Avenue to Sundance and Healy Trail, helped H.E. Sibbald put up hitching post for packing competition, 12 miles rode.
January 28th - Stormy, cold
To office and about town, to shack at horse pasture, took saddles and blankets etc. to wardens' storeroom, helped put up teepees on Banff Avenue, 5 miles car.

January 29th - Fine, cold

At packing competition in forenoon, Cave Avenue to Sundance and Healy Trails, west on Auto Road to sucker spring, 14 miles rode.

February 1921
February 2nd - Cloudy

Sundance and Healy Trail to Healy Lodge with Bill Peyto's outfit to catch wolverine and lynx for Zoo, 12 miles rode, broke trail.

February 7th - Cloudy, windy

Sundance Canyon and Healy Creek Trail, gathered up teepee poles on Banff Avenue and took teepees to owners, 10 miles rode and walked.

February 14th - Snow, east wind

To station, about town, at garage and office, made out reports, put same in storekeeper's office, went to Anthracite with McAulay, 12 miles auto and walked.

February 21st - Fine

West on track to mileage 86, Auto Road to 7 mile spring, back by track, to Buffalo Park in afternoon, catching sheep and goat for Vancouver, 20 miles auto, speeder and snowshoeing.

February 25th - Chinook

Bankhead and Anthracite and Spray River with vet, took reading of water gauge for Sanson, 24 miles auto.

February 26th - Chinook

To office forenoon, west on Auto Road to 1st Lake, east to Canmore with Chief Warden to bring vet and Fyfe to Banff, 35 miles auto and saddle horse.

February 28th

Bankhead and Anthracite with vet on inspection of cattle, to Spray River in afternoon, 22 miles auto.

March 1921
March 1st - Fine

East to Canmore and Kananaskis with vet and Fyfe

inspecting and inoculating dairy cows, 64 miles by car, home 9:30.

March 3rd - Fine

Bankhead and Anthracite with vet and Fyfe inspecting cows, 22 miles auto.

March 4th - Stormy

East to Canmore, Gap, Exshaw and Kananaskis with vet to inspect cattle - left 8:30, 64 miles auto, home 9 p.m.

March 9th - Snow, all day from east

Packed up buffalo heads and scalps and shipped to Edmonton, to Hot Springs and Cave and Basin with National Cash Register man, auto 7 miles, walked 3 miles.

March 10th - Cold, east wind

At garage helping Pepper overhaul car no. 3, walked 3 miles.

March 11th - Cold, east wind

At garage overhauling car, saw Wilson boy and inquired about young deer found by him and found it to be away on side of Tunnel, apparently just laid down and died of natural causes, 4 miles walked.

March 14th - Stormy

At park catching and crating sheep and goat for New York, drove 5 miles.

March 22nd - Mild

To station and stable, took up mountain lion to Zoo, shipped lumber to Lake Louise, took Walcott mare to Buffalo Park, home along track, 8 miles car and walked.

March 23rd - Mild

To station, expecting mountain lion by express, west on track to 3rd Lake, looking for six shooter lost by me on Friday, did not find it, about town and at garage and stable, 6 or 7 miles speeder and walked.

March 24th - Cold

At station looking for mountain lion, Cave Avenue and Sundance Canyon, to park and counted sheep, trimmed feet of Walcott's mare, 14 miles rode and walked.

March 26th - Cloudy, east wind

To station for mountain lion and took to Zoo, east to Canmore with Inspector Ryan and Warren to try man for breaking leg of deer, man threw at deer to clear it away after it had knocked child down, 65 miles auto.

March 28th - West wind, mild Easter Monday

West on Auto Road to Mount Edith Pass, returned oats to west, went to Spray and took water readings for Sanson, 10 miles rode.

March 29th - Mild

To Spray River, to station with gasoline for speeder, took Warren to Massive to see telephone gang working east, snow very deep, 20 miles speeder.

March 30th - Mild

At Zoo and repaired monkey cages with wire netting, west on Auto Road to 3 mile board repairing new telephone line with Warren, 8 miles rode and walked.

March 31st - Mild

At Zoo and moved coyotes, to station after lynx from Field, animal had broken leg when found in cage, shipped roofing etc. to Lake Louise, took Stewart to Cave and Basin and Hot Springs to collect money, 10 miles auto.

April 1921

April 7th - Cloudy

West on Auto Road to 7 mile spring repairing Banff-Castle line, met Naylor and Curren at 7 mile spring, 14 miles rode - 9 hours.

April 8th - Mild

West on track to Castle Mountain, to Anthracite, took engineer Childe to look at pier on Bow Bridge, 50 miles with McAulay, speeder and car.

April 12th - Fine

Cave Avenue and Sundance and Healy Trail to Healy Cabin, cut out telephone east of cabin and brought in toboggan - spare phone etc., back to Cave and Basin with clothes for Bill Noble, 14 miles rode, 3 miles auto.

April 15th - Showery

About town, getting horses for Duke's party in forenoon and afternoon, 4 or 5 miles rode.

April 16th - Fine

Buffalo Park and about town, getting saddle horses ready for Duke of Devon and party, to station and horse pasture, 4 or 5 miles walked.

April 19th - Fair

Took Childe and Archibald to see bridge, saw Naylor, helped Curren on shack in pasture, 44 miles speeder and walked.

April 21st - Cloudy

At Zoo with Warren to move coyotes, got bitten on side of head by small one, went to hospital and got wound cauterized, then moved coyotes, went to park in afternoon and caught sheep and shipped same on east bound express to Texas, 10 hours, 12 miles auto and walked.

April 23rd - Cloudy

Took Curren to storeroom to mark blankets, at garage, Chief's office, west on track to Castle Mountain with grub for Archibald's gang, 45 miles speeder and walked.

April 25th - Fair

To Forty Mile Creek, showing Warren how to run fire unit, at garage fixing up hose etc., 8 hours misc., 4 miles walked.

April 26th - Fair

To station with Chief Warden to ship express to Kananaskis and saddle to Prettie at Calgary, shipped bed to Phillips at Lake Louise, helping Curren put in shelves and straighten up garage, 6 miles auto and walked.

May 1921

May 1st - Fine

West on Auto Road to Mount Edith Pass and 4 mile board, Buffalo Park road, 10 miles rode, saw 52 mule deer in 2 miles on Auto Road - 21 on one bank, lots of sheep.

May 2nd - Stormy

Bankhead with vet, inspected cow butchered by Wright,

went to Canmore and butchered two more, inspected herd at Bankhead Dairy, 40 miles auto.

May 3rd - Fair

East to Exshaw and Kananaskis with vet and Fyfe, butchered milk cow at Exshaw, 56 miles auto.

May 4th - Showery

At garage and Zoo in forenoon - helping catch grizzly bear to get tooth out, to Bankhead Dairy in afternoon with vet and Fyfe, butchered cow, 10 miles auto.

May 6th - Fine

West on Auto Road to Castle Mountain, took Mumford to 4 mile board to pile brush, went to Castle for gophers, to Spray in afternoon with Curren, rolled up fire hose, west on Auto Road to 3 mile board at night for Mumford, 50 miles auto.

May 9th - Cloudy, rain forenoon and evening

West on Auto Road to Johnston Canyon with Mr. Sibbald and Mumford, helped Mumford make camp, car had loose connection, had to leave on side of road, came to town after dark with A. Keith - 11:15, had men burning brush 1 mile west of Banff, to station and about town, 35 miles auto.

May 10th - Showery, hailstorm afternoon

West on Auto Road to 15 mile with Capel and Reo truck, towed in car no. 3, fixed up Reo fire truck and took men to 5 mile board, gang had culvert dug out, could not get across, came back to 4 mile board and burnt brush, 40 miles truck and 12 miles no. 7 auto.

May 12th - Cloudy, some snow

Working on car no. 3 in forenoon, out to Bankhead and to Buffalo Park for meat for Zoo, to Canmore with Chief Warden in afternoon with wire etc., for Latam to repair line Canmore to White Man Pass, 40 miles car no. 20.

May 13th - Fine

Took Mrs. Fee's baggage to station, took saddles to pasture for wardens from Field, working on truck no. 3, 5 miles auto.

May 14th - Fair

West on Auto Road to 7 mile spring, put out salt for sheep, also walked over to track, horse belonging to E. Bird got broken leg caused by train no. 2 last night, got outfit ready to catch suckers but got call to fire near Hatchery, let town brigade connect to hydrant - 1 acre, 18 miles auto (nos. 20 and 7).

May 17th - Fine

East on Auto Road to Morley, north to Ghost River and Aura Ranger Station with seed oats for Caine at Red Deer, met fire auto at Latam's, repaired tire and drove same, home 10 p.m., 148 miles car no. 20.

May 18th - Fine

To station for mechanic's baggage, getting car no. 7 running, to Anthracite for bridge gang, Capel not back, 12 miles auto.

May 19th - Fine, hot and dry

Around garage fixing up pumps and working around garage, 4 or 5 miles walked, set pheasant eggs (13).

May 21st - Rain

Around garage altering tailboard for new car, sent pump to Lake Louise and received one from Lake Louise, put two more pheasant eggs under hen, 3 or 4 miles walked.

The Banff Crag & Canyon - May 21st 1921

To Eliminate Mosquitoes

The government is taking prompt measures this season to eliminate as far as possible the mosquito nuisance which drove so many people away from the village last summer.

N. B. Sanson has charge of the work of spreading oil on ponds and bodies of stagnant water, the coating oil having been found to be most effective remedy for preventing the breeding of mosquitoes.

With "Heinie," the captured German pony, bearing the cans of oil, Mr. Sanson is giving a thorough coating of oil to all still water and visitors will not be obliged to work overtime this summer in fighting the pesky skeeters.

May 24th - Fine

West on Auto Road to Mount Edith Pass, west in afternoon to sucker spring with Chief Warden to locate fire on track - reported by Sanson, pile of ties and trash, 18 miles auto.

May 30th - Fine

Helped Warren pack up, killed sheep for Zoo, changing tires on wheels of fire car, got call at night to fire at Garbage Grounds, found rubbish burning.

May 31st - Fine

Changing tires on fire car and went up Spray River to point where fire was supposed to be, went to Canmore - fire reported at 8 miles on track - old ties, made trips to Canmore afternoon and night, connected hose to standpipe on Golf Links and soaked fire at Nuisance Grounds and left hose on all day, 65 miles cars nos. 3 and 20.

June 1921

June 1st - Cloudy, rain at night

To park and Golf Links and around garage, fixing pump and mending Ford tires, caught sheep at park and turned out on Golf Links, helped Bill Peyto catch horses and pack up to go to Spray Lakes, 14 miles auto.

June 3rd - Fine, King's birthday

Cave Avenue, Sundance Canyon with Chief Warden, to falls and Spray River, went to Lake Minnewanka for McAulay, killed sheep at park and hauled same to Zoo, to sucker hole and caught fish for bears.

June 4th - Fine

To 7 mile hill east with man and camp for McAulay, to Loop and shot sheep that had busted leg, baited carcass for coyotes, 21 miles auto.

June 7th - Fair

West on Auto Road to Baker Creek with Chief Warden and telephone gang, 60 miles auto, to Hot Springs after bear with trap on foot.

June 10th - Fine

Went to Golf Links and hung up telephone line with Fuller,

at garage in forenoon, 3 miles auto no. 7.

June 12th - Fine

To 5 ½ mile creek to fire - 2 acres, with 4 wardens, McAulay and 2 road gang, 11 miles car no. 7 - 6 hours fighting fire.

June 13th - Rain forenoon, fine afternoon

Around town and to river drivers' camp in Loop in evening, helping Curren gather up outfit and grub and took same to wardens' shack in pasture in afternoon, at Zoo at 8:00, killed polar bear, 12 miles auto.

June 17th - Fair

Around garage forenoon, to Buffalo Park - gathered up horses and changed to lower field and separated Mr. Walcott's from government horses, Sundance Canyon and Spray River south of CP Hotel, 20 miles auto and rode.

June 20th - Fine

Helped C. Fuller get outfit ready for Lake Louise, about Buffalo Park, fixed up buffalo bull calf, gathered up supplies etc. for Chief Warden to take with men to Lake Louise, changed tire on car no. 7, repaired spare, notified Mr. Wood of fire 10 miles east, went east to 7 mile hill, saw fire appeared to be in Loop, returned to Loop and fire across Bow, went to 12 mile board for Archibald's gang and took across river to Loop, took back part of gang to Banff, home - 1 a.m., 10 miles car no. 3, 76 miles car no. 7.

June 21st - Fine

To Hoodoos and Upper Anthracite Road - 5 a.m., took men to Archibald's camp 12 miles east, got men at yard and sent them to fire to meet Warren, also sent Latam with lunch for men, took tank off car no. 7 to be repaired, went to Lake Louise with Chief Warden and brought car to Banff, 80 miles car no. 3, 36 miles car no. 7.

June 23rd - Hot

Hoodoos trail to scene of fire on Cascade Flats, looking for possible spark of fire, at garage, put gas tank on car no. 7, went to Loop for 1 ½ inch hose, hurry up call to fire on east side of Rundle, 1 mile below Loop drive, came to Banff for pumping unit etc., fire travelling in crowns, 35 miles car no. 7.

June 24th - Fine, rain at night

5 a.m. to fire with men, ran pump all day, stayed all night, to town one trip, 17 hours, 15 miles car and walked.

June 25th - Showery

At fire on east side of Rundle opposite of Cascade River, helped put tools etc. across river, came to town - 17 hours, 7 miles car and walked.

June 27th - Fine, strong west wind

To 7 mile hill and 12 mile camp on Cascade, carrying tools etc. used at fire to road, brought to Banff and took shovels to Archibald's at night, reported to Chief condition of fire as seen from across river, got man from McAulay at 10 a.m. till six, 38 miles car no. 7.

June 28th - Fine

East on Auto Road to Archibald's camp, got 2 men at 1 p.m. till 7:30 and one from McAulay at 10 a.m. - working on fire edges in moss, 35 miles car no. 7.

June 29th - Hot

East to road camp for 2 men, took Bill and Robert to fire [Editor's note - Bill Peyto and son Robert], also took back pump across river, got hose and pump etc., 10 hours, 24 miles car no. 20.

July 1921

July 5th - Some rain

East to Canmore, loaded up Latam's outfit and to Cochrane, then north to Harmattan by way of Cremona, 110 miles auto.

July 6th - Cloudy

Harmattan to Sundre then west to coal camp, east to Olds, got cars stuck in mud at coal camp, got Latam through then unloaded my load and went back to Olds for load of supplies for Latam, 70 miles car.

July 7th

Olds to Sundre then to Boundary Cache Ranger Station and

made round trip to coal camp, 64 miles car.

July 8th - Fine

From Ranger Station on Red Deer to Cochrane by way of Sundre, Harmattan and Cremona.

July 9th - Fine

At Cochrane fixing up car in forenoon, west to Banff.

July 12th - Showery

Put hose out to dry that had been brought from fire on Mount Rundle while I was north - left in a pile in garage, 22 lengths, 2800 feet, rolled up 700 feet that was already out and washed up fire truck, 4 or 5 miles walked.

July 14th - Fine

Sundance Canyon and Hot Springs and Spray Avenue, to Lady MacDonald Cottage after bear in afternoon and back at night, bear came out and was shot by Bill Peyto with a 303 pointed bullet. As this bear did not fall at once Mrs. West Jones and her husband declared it was not touched and that we had gone there with orders not to shoot this bear but only scare it, said she would write Ottawa and get us discharged and in fact spoke in a very insulting manner for one that was supposed to be a lady, just because we would not go and sit in the house or on the veranda. We took the only position from which it was possible to do any shooting as there were so many people walking through the woods. B. Peyto stayed near house all night as they would not be told the bear would not come back.

July 15th - Fine

Rolled up hose and left B. Peyto to tie it up, went with Mr. Sibbald looking for bear at camp in Loop, and to Hot Springs, went to camp at Golf Links with Bill Peyto and shot bear that had been molesting camp. Mr. Wood came along and evidently to show his authority said, "Is this the right bear?" We told him that we did not ask the bear as he had already been in one tent, he said he was not going to have them shot, Chief Sibbald came along and was satisfied so we shouldn't worry.

161

July 16th - Fine

Went to Loop and got bear hide and salted same, shipped material to Lake Louise and grub for Red Deer Trail, to Hot Springs and Alpine Club looking for marauding bears at night, saw that fire truck was ready for call.

July 20th - Hot, some showers in spots

Around yard and garage forenoon, east to Canmore in afternoon to fire above mines, fire burning since last fall underground, 35 miles auto.

July 25th - Fine

To Buffalo Park and caught up horse for W. Fails to take to Canmore for Tabuteau to take to Kananaskis, Sundance Canyon and Hot Springs.

July 26th - Cloudy, stormy afternoon

West on Auto Road to Lake Louise, took rubber washers for hose to Phillips who was at fire at mileage 112, cut trees off trail east of Massive, reported bad culvert at Sawback to Edwards.

July 27th - Fine

Loop and Golf Links putting up cardboard fire signs (Save the Forest) and tested out telephone, helped catch horses and pack up to go to Spray Lakes and issued outfit.

July 28th - Fine

Gathered up horses from buffalo pasture and took to upper end of big meadows, helped Reeves fix up phones in Chief's office and testing howlers east and west, up Forty Mile and Whiskey Creeks to 1st Lake to see what smoke was from, found mosquito gang's dinner fire.

July 29th - Fine

Unpacking and checking boxes from Ottawa, shipping military saddles to Jasper Park, hauled supplies and hay to horse pasture for Curren, tested pumping unit.

July 30th - Fine

East to Kananaskis to butcher cow belonging to Mrs. Staple, brought meat to Zoo, put new batteries in Canmore Lodge phone, clutch on red car no. 20 would not grip on hill at Exshaw, had to come to Banff for truck to pull car no. 20

home - arrived home 1:30, not my fault clutch was dry, 80 miles autos nos. 20 and 12 and private car.

August 1921`
August 2nd - Cloudy
Filled up tanks on car no. 7 with gas and tested tires for air, drove Chief Warden to Middle Springs camp looking for bear, went back after dinner and then to CP Hotel and Loop and back to Middle Springs, no bear around, 15 miles auto.
August 3rd - Rain
Cave Avenue and Loop to Garbage Grounds, took bear from Chief's house to dump, went to rifle range with Chief Warden, Dr. Atkin and Fowles to try out their guns, 10 miles auto.
August 4th - Cloudy
About town forenoon, to Lake Louise in afternoon - home 11 p.m., 18 hours, gathered up outfit for Chief Warden and Supt., took horses to Mount Edith Pass, helped them pack, put up signs on Auto Road west of Lake Louise, saw Mumford and Phillips, 80 miles auto.
August 5th - Fine
Helping Curren pack horses, took pump to river and ran to loosen up shaft, to Sundance Canyon in afternoon, put up "Save the Forest" signs, fixed up pumps in garage, took off long exhaust pipes and cut to short ones, 12 miles auto.
August 7th - Fine
Walked through pasture up towards dam, picked raspberries.
August 12th - Cloudy
To Canmore at fire laying out hose etc. with Bill Peyto, Fuller away looking for 5 horses, 35 miles auto - home 7 p.m.
August 13th - Fine, hot
At Canmore pumping water to bog, put fire out, maybe it will burn up again, brought back part of hose, home 7 p.m., got call at 11 p.m. to go with Chief and Warren to fire at Kootenay on Hawk Creek near Auto Road, left 12 p.m., 35 miles auto.

August 14th - Hot, cold during night

Arrived at Hawk Creek 4:30 a.m., Warren went to Bird's camp where fire was reported, saw fire more than halfway up mountain, Naylor reported fire small, one tree apparently having been struck by lightning, returned to Banff, 100 miles auto.

August 21st - Showery

3 a.m. to fire at Sanitarium Steam Laundry, to Nuisance Grounds, fire reported or smoke blowing down from garbage, 10 miles auto and walked.

August 23rd - Fine

At garage working on car, called out at 10 p.m. to go east and meet Bigler with Lawyer Lafferty, found Super's car in fence at Anthracite. Returned to Banff, saw Bigler talking to Super who asked me to drive Bigler home, he (Bigler) being drunk, but he wanted to go and get his car. I hunted around for Casey Jones, Bigler helped but was unable to find him, saw Jones and Bigler taking car in about 7 a.m. Wood told me that Lafferty was drunk in court, I also heard he was in town at 9:30 but did not get to Police Court till 10:30.

August 27th - Fine

To Bankhead and Cascade Trail with supplies for Wright to take to Panther (Windy) Cabin, helped him pack lumber, at garage fixing gas line on car no. 24, went to Golf Links looking for dog chasing sheep, also got 200 feet of hose for Thompson, took supplies to corral for Curren.

August 29th - Fair

To pasture with nails etc. for Curren, told Bill Peyto to watch which way Amoss went, to Mount Edith Pass to head him off for not registering, went to Massive to locate smoke on south side (smudge at Simpson's horse camp) took R. Edwards to 6 mile board to put out clearing fire.

August 30th - Fine

Took HES to station, then took supplies to Bankhead for Wright to take to Windy Cabin, working in garage forenoon, 12 miles auto.

August 31st - Showery

About town and stable, got call to go to Canmore to small fire, took big pump and pumped for several hours - 900 feet, everything okay when left, 35 miles auto no. 7, asked Super for load of rails to build pen for mountain goat (newly caught), small load of heavy rails were sent to park.

September 1921

September 1st - Fair

Spray Valley to Eau Claire camp with Bill Peyto (no corral built yet) and loaded up 2 female and 2 kid goats, turned out two horses in pasture and put hose out to dry, told J. B. Harkin how I had to dry hose and he told Stewart that he ought to build a tower, 18 miles saddle horse and auto.

September 2nd - Cloudy

Got saddle horses shod, to lower Buffalo Park and rounded up horses, took same to upper meadows west of Banff, took supplies to Bankhead for Wright, to Hot Springs with Bill Peyto, shot black bear and took carcass to Nuisance Grounds, to station at night.

September 5th - Cloudy

At office forenoon, to upper meadows in afternoon catching horses with Warden Naylor.

September 8th - Cloudy

At garage working on car no. 26, took Stewart to Hot Springs, Cave and Basin and Golf Links to collect cash.

September 12th - Stormy

To Zoo with Bill Peyto and killed bear, took same to Garbage Grounds, worked on car no. 26.

September 13th - Snow

Got car no. 7 ready and waited orders to take to Hot Springs, at garage in forenoon, at Spray River and Golf Links in afternoon, working on car no. 26 and running pump on big truck for Commissioner Harkin and Supts. Bevan and Russell, put hose out to dry and brought home hose from Garbage Grounds.

September 16th - Fair, rain at night
Working on car no. 26, took horses to upper meadows, took Bill Peyto along Sundance Road and left him watching salt lick for poachers, while hunting for horses in pasture found place where someone had put out salt in several places.

September 18th - Fair, rain at night
West on Auto Road to Johnston Canyon and return, west to Lake Louise and Moraine Camp, took Bill Peyto up to kill off bear, patrolling Johnston Canyon and Hillsdale - took family for a ride.

September 19th - Rain
Lake Louise to Banff, to Buffalo Park, moved buffalo from Zoo to park, took fire pump to Canmore to fire at mouth of old mine, started pump and left in charge of Wardens Fuller and James, 78 miles auto nos. 24 and 7.

September 20th - Cloudy
West on Auto Road to Castle and south to Vermilion Summit and Black's camp, returned to Vermilion Cabin, repairing car no. 3 - 4 hours, helped move telephone gang camp, 50 miles auto no. 24.

September 21st - Showery
Vermilion Cabin to Banff, repaired spring on car no. 24 and rolled up hose, brought in dishes from Mumford's camp, and left stove at Massive, Warren phoned that we had to take his horses out of stable, 40 miles auto no. 24.

September 22nd - Fair
West to Massive with outfit for H. Fuller, at garage in afternoon, changed tires on car no. 24 and took freight to station for Vermilion telephone gang.

September 23rd - Showery
At garage, changed tires on car no. 26, east to Canmore Lodge with stove etc. for Warden James and brought stove to Banff, auto, sealed 44.40 Martin for Ernest Stenton.

September 26th - Rain
At garage and repaired car no. 26, shipping and packing supplies etc. for Latam - Red Deer, auto.

September 28th - Rain

Lower Buffalo Park and killed horse for Zoo, got horses ready for Engineer Mitchell to take to Spray Lakes, hauled old timber from old gravel pit to fix place for my horse.

October 1921

October 1st - Fine

To park with pump and hose, watered yak in corrals, fixing up stable for my horse at Bill Peyto's, 8 miles auto.

October 3rd - Fine, windy

To park, loaded yak, left Banff at 7 p.m. to Calgary with yak for Wainwright, Calgary at 1:30 a.m., 90 miles auto and train.

October 4th - Cloudy

Left Calgary at 5:30 a.m., Calgary to Wetaskiwin at 9:15 via Red Deer with yak, freight train.

October 5th

Left Wetaskiwin at 4:30, to Camrose at 7 a.m.

October 6th - Cloudy, cold

Left Camrose at 7 a.m., arrived Wainwright at 4 p.m.

October 7th - Fine

Left Wainwright at 7:30 p.m., arrived Edmonton at 11:15 p.m.

October 8th - Cloudy

Left Edmonton at 12:35 a.m., arrived Calgary at 7 a.m., left Calgary at 7:55 a.m., arrived Banff at 11:45, met George Harrison and Frayne coming from Sundre, also Harold Deegan.

October 12th - Fair

Took gasoline and oil to Vermilion for telephone gang, met N.B. Sanson at Massive and Warden Fuller on way to Banff, told him I had seen lost horses near Castle Mountain.

October 15th - Cloudy

Hauled meat from lower pasture to Zoo, took oats to Naylor at Castle and brought telephone gang to Banff, took Bill Peyto to Massive to bring in horses.

October 16th - Cloudy

To Golf Links in afternoon with Supt. and shot four horn sheep that had broken back - 2 hours.

October 18th - Fine

To park and loaded up hay on auto, took same to Castle, helped Chief Warden lay out foundations for Castle Cabin, took pack horses from stable to pasture, 45 miles auto.

October 20th - Rain

Unloaded team from Yoho off car, to Chief's office, west to Castle with hay for Vermilion, turned out team in field, 40 miles auto, got orders from H. E. Sibbald to take phone out of Johnston Canyon Tea Room. When I went there I found the door unlocked and the front door broken open, I nailed up the front door and locked the back door after removing the phone.

October 22nd - Fair

Killed horse for Zoo, to Chief's office and took horses from horse pasture to Buffalo Park, reported to Duncan McCowan that Johnston Canyon Tea Room had been broken into, he said that Constable Warke had reported it open.

October 24th - Cloudy

West to Castle Mountain and south to Vermilion Summit and Marble Canyon with engineer Welby to take levels of lots laid out by team.

October 25th - Cloudy

Packed coal to Sulphur Mountain for Sanson with Bill Peyto.

October 27th - Fair

Built corral at Golf Links and caught sheep and took to Buffalo Park - 50 head, found carcass of bull elk apparently killed through fighting - partly eaten by coyotes, hide and scalp spoiled, no time to remove head - too busy with sheep.

October 29th - Stormy

Took supplies and roofing to Massive for Red Earth Creek, took cement to Castle and helped load lumber for Lake Louise, got last of grub from Bill Peyto and 8 blankets, 2 shovels, some roofing and tar paper. Warren told me Warden Fuller would go help Bill Peyto as it was too much for one man with several head of horses.

October 31st - Stormy, snow

To Massive and return to Golf Links and horse pasture, took stove etc. to Bill Peyto at Massive, fed horses and repaired corral.

November 1921

November 2nd

To Golf Links and side of Mount Rundle trying to run in sheep, but they could climb too well, to horse pasture branding and numbering sheep for Red Deer, 10 miles saddle horse and auto.

November 4th - Fine

Left Banff, got as far as Harmattan on way to Red Deer valley via Cochrane and Sundre, had one blow out and broke small spring under truck, 150 miles auto.

November 5th - Fine

Getting spring repaired in forenoon, went to coal camp in afternoon, had trouble with brakes, 25 miles auto.

November 6th - Snow all day

Fixed up brakes in forenoon, went to Logan's Ranch, car not working good.

November 7th - Snow, cold

Laid over at Logan's Ranch fixing brakes etc. on car.

November 8th - Cloudy, rain at night

Laid over at Bob Logan's, 4 miles auto.

November 9th - Cloudy, rain at night

Car not working, unable to move at times, went as far as Cremona, roads very heavy, had to get car hauled out of mud, had to camp at foot of hill in willows overnight, 24 miles auto.

November 10th - Fair

Got hauled up hills, got to telephone line and made up one's mind to either advance the timer or break it as it was on so solid, managed to move it, had to buy coal oil, could not get gas, after awhile met a man who gave us 3 gallons on condition we got his car filled in Cochrane, got to Cochrane 6:30 p.m., 48 miles car.

November 11th - Cloudy

Cochrane to Banff, reported to Chief Warden Sibbald, 85 miles car.

November 12th - Cloudy

Chasing sheep at Golf Links and Spray River and Mount Rundle, shot two old rams and brought a male angora to town - with Bill Peyto and Naylor, 12 miles saddle horse.

November 18th - Cold, 21 below

Took gang to Sundance Canyon in forenoon, helped skin out 4 Rocky Mountain sheep, took heads and hides to Belmore Browne's residence on Spray Avenue for James Simpson, went for men at night, 20 miles auto.

November 20th - Cold

Through moose pasture to Tote Road and Forty Mile Creek and horse pasture, saw work mare walking very lame, looked at foot and found her to have nail running straight up through frog, went to house and got pliers and pulled nail out, lots of puss and blood came out. No feed around and horses appeared to be hungry, I fed them over fence, 5 or 6 miles walked.

November 22nd - Snow

Took lumber to shack for Curren, took Warren to park and I worked in garage, shipped boxes to Phillips and hose to Supt. - Yoho Park, 10 miles auto.

November 25th - Snow, warmer

To Sundance Canyon with gang and brought them home at night, got saddles from station for E.W. Peyto and Curren, took to shack in pasture, to Loop and Garbage Grounds, 24 miles saddle horse and auto.

November 30th - Mild

Took men to canyon, gathered up supplies and shipped to Fuller at Morley, and took oats to James in Canmore and supplies for Warden Curren to take to Gap and Boundary Cabins, went for men at night, 45 miles auto.

December 1921

December 6th - Fair, west wind, Dominion General Election
Took men to Canyon Road at 10 a.m. after they had voted,
fetched home at night with all tools, met Bill Peyto walking
to town from Simpson Summit, drove him to town.

December 8th - Fair
Sacking oats and shipping hay to Naylor at Castle, west on
Auto Road to Mount Edith Pass - 5 hours, set traps for lynx
on pass, 12 miles auto and saddle horse.

December 11th - Rain
Called up by several people to tell me about a deer laying at
the corner of Wolf and Muskrat Streets, took horse and
toboggan and hauled carcass away (badly bruised up from
fighting - blood in one eye).

December 13th - Colder
To Spray River with men and brought them back at night,
took carcass of deer meat out to 1st Lake for coyote bait,
saw Ben Holbrow prowling along creek, picked up some
traps and put on his doorstep.

December 16th - Fair
To Spray River and Loop with men and brought them back
at night, Cave Avenue and Sundance and Healy Trail,
picked up Bill Peyto's outfit, and caught lynx in trap.

December 20th - Cold, 45 below
To government yards and wardens' storeroom, to station
and shipped furniture to Warden Phillips at Lake Louise,
took Fyfe to station and Buffalo Park.

December 30th - Fair, snow early morning
Went to Canmore with J. Warren, west on Auto Road to
crossings of creek to look for bridge site, 38 miles auto and
saddle horse.

December 31st - Fair
To office and Zoo, killed diseased monkey, went to park and
caught up team and got shod in afternoon, went to horse
pasture and saw fence was alright to keep elk out around
hay.

Jack Warren and Walter Peyto with grizzly - 1920.
Whyte Museum of the Canadian Rockies. V573 NA66-2191.

Cave and Basin - 1920. Whyte Museum of the Canadian
Rockies.
V263 NA71-3547.

Banff Station - 1920. Whyte Museum of the Canadian Rockies.
V263 NA71-3513.

Bankhead Station - 1920. Whyte Museum of the Canadian
Rockies. V573 NA66-360.

Nineteen Twenty Two

January 1922
January 1st - Stormy
Home all day - 7:30 got telephone call asking if I had any idea of three boys supposed to have gone west on skis and to return via Healy Creek Trail, notified Warren, was preparing to go with Bill Peyto when call came that they had arrived home but had not gone in direction they said but around Squaw Mountain, told their father to warn them to either go the way they said next time or make shorter trip and return earlier than intended.
January 2nd - Cold, holiday
Home all day, Warren phoned me that I would have to take men to Bankhead with truck. I told him I would prefer to have the truck that I had been driving which was given to Mason by Wood as the only other trucks had something wrong. I called the mechanic's attention to same in case anything broke.
January 5th - Bright and cold
To Bankhead with men, to Edwards' gang with tools, to Buffalo Park to get work teams and put in upper pasture, horses all taken up track to Banff Station, took Warren and Supt. to station, shipped supplies to Hislop at Gap. I went to Bankhead for men at night.
January 6th - Fair
Took gang to Bankhead, west on Auto Road to sucker spring, to Edwards' bridge gang and 3 mile board, took ladder from my own house, to Bankhead at night after men, truck broke down near Bankhead, phoned to garage to get another truck to tow mine to town and take men in - 10 hours, got home 6:30. I had called both J.R. Warren and Bigler's attention to the thump in this truck when changing gears on Tuesday morning.
January 7th - Cloudy
Took men to lake road in Warren's car, then took Warren out to look at well, he did not go down as Harrison wanted

him to, went out again at night and brought men to town, car on the bum, met Capel towing car no. 27 from Canmore, 35 miles auto.

January 8th - Cloudy, mild

West on Auto Road to Mount Edith Pass - 2 hours, Warren phoned that a buffalo had been killed, went with B. Peyto and cut off head and took insides out, phoned Warren to have team there tomorrow morning to pull carcass out of field, met Supt. at stable, told him that buffalo had been killed, he said, "Oh well, that will be one less to feed."

January 15th - Fair, cool east wind

Home all day, got Bill Peyto's horse from stable for him to go and set trap for mountain lion.

January 16th - Snow, east wind

To Sundance Creek and Rainy Bay with bridge gang and brought them home at night, to Buffalo Park to tell McTrowe to pull switch on line to dam, to Loop looking for lame deer and intern camp after tin to put in crates, to Bankhead well site with Warren, picked out new site, 33 miles auto.

January 19th - Cold

To Bankhead with men, took load of lumber out - 3 hours, got buffalo head and scalp from park and took to stores, took desk from stores to Warren's office and other one back to stores, after men at night, 2 hours - at fire on Marten Street.

January 27th - Snow

Auto Road forenoon and night, took gang to bridge and brought them back with all tools, to Brewster upper stable with Warren, got pack bags etc. for competition, hauled saddles etc. from shack at pasture to wardens' storeroom, made up packs for competition.

January 28th - Cold

About town and garage forenoon, moving Bickle fire truck to another place in garage, Warren says Supt.'s orders and to block up and let air out of tires, this makes it useless in case of fire at Hot Springs or elsewhere where there are not

175

hydrants - as intended by orders from H.E. Sibbald last fall, at the best this car could not be got out under half an hour in the day time and when all the trucks are out, at night it would mean an hour by the time we got the trucks out of the way, at packing and camping contest.

January 29th - Cold, some snow

Took horse and cutter to Lougheed's afternoon.

January 30th - Cold

About town forenoon, to office, to wood chopping contest, to Buffalo Park in afternoon.

February 1922

February 1st - Cold

Took men to work at Rainy Bay, brought in tools for Edwards' gang, took Indians to ski jump in afternoon (supposed to be on holidays).

February 3rd - Cool

At carnival.

February 4th - Fair

Went to Mount Edith Pass, saw tracks of mountain lion, lost one trap, saw Bill Peyto at night about traps, off duty.

February 6th - Fair

Helped take down teepees for carnival outfit, taking lights off palace, Bill Peyto went up to pass and set traps for lions.

February 7th - Cold

To Chief's office to see about loading sheep, met Mr. Hodges from Montana (Dixon) bison range.

February 11th - Cold, off duty

Went to Auto Road to Mount Edith Pass, met Bill Peyto, looked at traps but saw no sign in pass of fresh tracks of mountain lion.

February 12th to February 26th - Cold

Off duty.

February 21st - Cold

West on Auto Road to Mount Edith and west to 6 mile sand hill with Bill Peyto looking for tracks of lion crossing from south side of valley.

March 1922
March 4th - Snow
West on Tote Road to Mount Edith Pass and 4 mile board, Squaw Mountain and old Tote Road to Forty Mile Creek crossing, saw 23 deer between mile boards 3 and 4, 14 miles rode.
March 8th - Fair
At garage and stores, got car no. 10 running and gathered up supplies and shipped to Galvin at Castle Mountain, drove Warren to Bankhead Cabin in afternoon, Spray Avenue to Grant's gang.
March 9th - Fair
Spray Avenue and west along track and side of 1st Lake, took gang in to burn brush cut by mosquito bunch, took Hungarian partridge killed by wires to Sanson at museum.
March 17th - Mild
To yard, saw gangs start out and went to Canmore with Steve Hope to sew up cut in horse where another horse had kicked him, met J. James and saw 2 elk, met Bill Peyto who sent Fuller up Squaw Mountain to look around, met Fuller who said he had found fresh kill on Squaw Mountain and had set trap, he tried to find Bill Peyto but set on his own.
March 18th - Mild, cloudy
To yard early afternoon, up tracks to brush burning gang, to stable to see lion brought off Squaw Mountain by Wardens Peyto and Fuller, to Spray Avenue, saw Grant getting saddle horse shod, saw Bill Peyto who said they had got lion - Fuller going up to look at trap without his rifle, rode and walked.
March 19th - Snow
Bankhead Road to horse pasture, across Whiskey Creek to where boys found fire in spruce grove, fire left by some boys seeking willows to make bows, walked.
March 24th - Mild
To yard, west on track to see brush burning gang, about station, across Whiskey Creek to car shed and Motor Road, put tools away, up to storeroom, saw McAulay about teams

to go to Bankhead with lumber, notified men to go to work Saturday, started T. Frayne to Bankhead.

March 29th - Mild

To yard forenoon, saw gang to Bankhead, home rest of day with neuralgia, voted on comm. in evening.

March 30th - Mild

To office and made up time books, about town forenoon and evening trying to locate talking crow, to hardware, to Bankhead with Warren.

April 1922

April 1st - Fair

To government stores and station, about town, to dentist and got teeth drawn, home in afternoon, walked.

April 5th - Fair

Took men to turn of Bankhead road and met Wright who took them on with horse and rig, Spray Avenue and Loop, car and saddle horse.

April 8th - Stormy

At government stores and garage, got material for Bankhead Cabin, took same to Bankhead in truck with Capel, about town in afternoon, phoned J. Warren that Bill Peyto's dog had treed a mountain lion.

April 10th - Stormy

At Zoo and Supt.'s house and stores, put up bird boxes at Zoo grounds and around Supt.'s house, moved wolf pups and coyotes at Zoo, walked.

April 11th - Stormy

At Hoodoos all day with movie outfit, rode.

April 13th - Fine

At Hoodoos with movie outfit, rode.

April 15th - Fair

At Bankhead and Minnewanka with movie outfit, met Warren, rode.

April 17th - Fine

To Upper Anthracite Road and Hoodoos and surrounding country with movie people - 8 hours, took pumping unit to

Fish Hatchery.

April 18th - Cloudy

At Fish Hatchery all day pumping water to inside tanks while repairs were being done to water main - 10 hours, Bill Peyto told me that he came near shooting big red setter dog on Upper Anthracite Road and had trouble with policemen (or boys).

April 19th - Fine

Upper Anthracite Road and Hoodoos and trail leading to Cascade Flats with movie outfit, rode.

April 21st - Fine

Bankhead and Lake Minnewanka with movie outfit, rode.

April 25th - Cloudy, stormy

Squaw Mountain with movie people who had to do a lot of shooting, rode.

April 26th - Clear

Spray Avenue and Spray River to Eau Claire camp with movie people and found kid goat in lavatory at camp - dead since fall, rode.

April 28th - Fine

West on Auto Road to Mount Edith Pass and four mile board and Spray Avenue to falls, visited Belmore Browne and saw paintings of sheep - only those given to curling club, got saddle horse shod.

April 29th - Fine

West on Auto Road to hills around 3 mile board with Bill Peyto looking for signs of mountain lion, supposed to have been seen last night, to Bankhead after Hislop and tools, car and saddle horse.

April 30th - Fine

Home all day, out in evening to try and rescue young deer off ice at falls, car.

May 1922

May 1st - Fine

Took Hislop and tools to station for Castle Mountain, burning grass and brush around Recreation Grounds, shot wolf at Zoo, took to Nuisance Grounds and got pump etc. from Fish Hatchery, car.

May 6th - Stormy

Working at garage forenoon, repairing cooling system on fire truck no. 23, Recreation Grounds and gathered up hose used and pump, took Warren to station, loaded up Jones' furniture, moved car no. 15 around and started same.

May 8th - Fine

At garage forenoon, west to Massive with speeder for Jones, at meadows west of town, burning off grass, took wife for a ride to see Mrs. Jones. Mrs. Jones washing the floor with a wash bowl, told her to use water bucket and I would bring her up another bucket and any other things she wanted for the house.

May 9th - Cloudy

To Loop and Golf Links repairing Banff-Canmore line near Nuisance Grounds, then working around garage on car no. 23, west on Auto Road after supper to Massive with supplies for Jones.

May 10th - Fair

At garage fixing up fire truck (23) and car no. 10, west on Auto Road with Bill Peyto who had reported to me of having seen smoke near Mount Edith Pass, found it to be from brush piles being burnt by road section men, met Mrs. Drummond Davis who told us she had seen a lion and had found an old dead sheep from which she had taken the head, Bill Peyto left me and walked down the Tote Road to investigate same, returning home across flats and reported same to J.R. Warren.

May 11th - Fine

Fixing up car no. 10 and working in garage putting snubbers on fire truck, west with Warren to ski jump to look at dead elk reported lying in bush, animal had been fighting in the winter and had not been found, did not have a large head.

May 12th - Fine

At garage, finished putting front snubbers on fire truck and got out saddles and boxes for mosquito gang, to Forty Mile Creek, with Mr. Sibbald, J.R. Warren and Mr. Prettie (a gas expert), testing out new type of fire pump with Fairbanks type.

May 22nd - Cloudy

Helped Warden E.W. Peyto pack outfit for Spray Lakes, working in garage putting springs on car no. 23, took car to Hatchery and starting pumping water into Hatchery - all night.

May 24th - Warm

Home forenoon, was called by Leacock that he had seen fire on north side of track at east switch, went and put out - about 6 square feet in moss and decayed timber, got another call and found one on north side of track near Banff Station - about 10 square feet in rotten logs.

May 25th - Warm

To garage and office, Cave Avenue, took outfit to Bankhead Station for Warren and took Warden Mumford to Lake Minnewanka to relieve Wright for a few days.

May 28th - Warm

Home forenoon, west on Auto Road to 3 mile board to fire smouldering in swamp with H.E. Sibbald, sent Mr. Wood to hunt up mosquito men who said they did not leave fire but that four ladies from the CPR Hotel orchestra were in there all day, took one of these men up and found tracks of women leading to this spot on north side of track with Warden E.W. Peyto, putting out fire in rotten timber and moss, took a lot of water - 9 hours fighting fire and investigation.

June 1922

June 2nd - Hot, smoky

To Buffalo Park moving horses and sorting out, to Buffalo Park in afternoon and took buffalo to town and put in Zoo, led and dragged him to town, west on Tote Road after supper to bring in and start car no. 10 which Warren could not, got out things for Phillips and put washer on wheel of car no. 7.

June 5th - Cloudy, cooler

To Castle Cabin with oil etc. for cabin, to Buffalo Park and station rounding up and shipping horses to Field, gave truck driver Capel two spark plugs for Phillips.

June 6th - Snow

To Buffalo Park, put men to work on corral instead of shearing sheep, to office - made out fire reports, went to Spray River and put up camp for Mumford.

June 10th - Cloudy

To station and unloaded stud horse and took to Buffalo Park, Banff to Minnewanka by car, brought back bunch of horses with E.W. Peyto and Tabuteau, lucky to run into Brewster men with old pack horses, ours were all green and some bridle wise.

June 13th - Fine

Taking outfit for Curren and Hislop to corral and helped Rodd catch horses and pack, west to 7 mile board with Warren looking for sheep with broken leg, took carcass to Zoo, hauled sheep to Zoo from park, to park and helped cut out horse for Ekstrom.

June 16th - Fine

At Zoo with Bickle pump, pumping out duck pond, got call to fire on Spray River near camp grounds - 1 hour, took new horses from pasture to Buffalo Park, rounded up bunch and picked out several and brought to upper pasture with E.W. Peyto, Fuller, J.R. Warren, killed horse for Zoo (old buffalo cripple).

June 17th - At stores and Buffalo Park, west to Massive to pasture and got horses for Jones, Galvin and Phillips, issued outfit for Galvin and Jones, gave same with horses to Galvin, took hay and oats to Massive and Zoo.

June 18th - Fine

Hot Springs forenoon, along Upper Anthracite Road and down on back side of Tunnel Mountain to rifle range, some rifle practice - engineers - no red flag out.

June 19th - Fair

Reported need of red flags to Supt., cleaned up garage and picked up old hose, mended several lengths, took Mr. Head to pasture and gave him saddle horse, went to Buffalo Park and told Fuller to take dog to lower Golf Links and look for mountain lion, Mr. Sibbald got message, told Warren who kept me at office fixing up fire reports and diary before sending me to get Fuller, out on north side of track and Forty Mile Creek investigating cause of smoke - only drifting from town.

June 20th - Cloudy

Saw E.W. Peyto starting out at 6 a.m., up to garage, to lumber yard and took lime to Zoo, took pump and old hose to Spray River with Fuller and showed him how to run pump and tested out hose, found some very leaky, west to 5 mile board with Mr. McTrowe and work horse, pack horse and my saddle horse and turned out in upper end of big meadow.

June 22nd - Fine

Helped Fuller pack outfit for Sanson for Simpson summit, west on Auto Road to Massive, took new stove, brought old stove from Massive and took to Mumford's camp, went to Buffalo Park with work sacks.

June 23rd - Fine

Along hills and up Squaw Mountain looking for sign of bear, took lumber to shack for Fuller and west on Auto Road to Castle and changed line, put on switches for south, east and west lines - home 9:30.

June 26th - Fine, hot

West on Auto Road to Castle, and south to Vermilion summit and Marble Canyon and mouth of Tokumm Creek, took man out to help Warden Ekstrom on telephone line, to Bankhead in evening.

June 27th - Hot

About town, to horse pasture, took supplies to Curren and Hislop and to Wright at Bankhead for trail gang, went to Observatory on Sulphur Mountain.

June 28th - Showery, heavy storm on summit at night

12:45 got call from J.R. Warren that Mr. Sibbald wanted two more pumps on Vermilion River, left Banff at 2:45, accompanied by H. Fuller, arrived Vermilion Bridge at 8:30 (had puncture), phoned Warren from summit to hold men ordered, worked all day at fire using pump, arrived Vermilion summit at 11:45 in big storm, 95 miles car and walked.

June 29th - Cloudy

Vermilion summit to Banff, home rest of day.

July 1922

July 1st - Hot, Dominion Day

At garage all day repairing and testing pumps nos. 2 and 5, took young fawn down to horse pasture to find its mother.

July 5th - Hot

At garage taking down pump no. 1 to see what had broken, found lower bearing no. 2 connecting rod pushed through crank case and shaft broken near flywheel, the bolt in no. 1 connecting rod was intact but had no wire through heads of bolts to keep them from getting loose and no sign of any having been put in, had mechanics from garage look at this as soon as I took off bottom crank case, Warden E.W. Peyto was in garage talking to me and saw me take engine apart. Note: this unit had not been taken down since return from Montreal last year.

July 8th - Showery

About garage and river testing pumps, west to Castle Mountain with mail and supplies for Jones, Galvin and E.W. Peyto.

July 17th - Hot and smoky

At Race Track in forenoon, pumping water for tanks to water track, rolled up hose in afternoon, working in garage, hauled meat to Zoo and hay to field and Bankhead office supplies, ball broke in front wheel, had to phone Warren to get me in from Bankhead, left car no. 10 out there.

July 19th - Hot, smoky

Got call from fire hall from Lou Hill that he had a call from Alpine Club that their ash pile was burning and they were getting scared and he had no way of getting there, ran up with Bickle and small pumping unit but got small hose from town and connected to their supply, they had no hose at club house at all - 2 hours, went to Bankhead and repaired car no. 10 and brought to town and worked around garage on pump, putting on carriers.

July 24th - Warm

Shipped insulators and wire to Castle Mountain for Kootenay, made two trips to Bankhead with supplies and outfit for Warren and Latam to take north, to garage and office fixing phone and putting together and painting unit no. 1.

July 25th - Cloudy

West on Auto Road and across track to upper end of big meadows with Fuller, cut place in river bank for horses to get water, found camp fire smouldering - 3 miles west of Banff on south side of track, ½ hour, put out by digging, to office and Recreation Grounds, picked out camp site for Norwegian and Lithuanian parsons, got time clocks and took to office and made out fire report.

July 29th - Hot and smoky

Mr. Sibbald and J.B. Harkin left for Kootenay fire, phoned Jones to come to Banff for horses, went to park and hauled load of wood for myself, got horses for Jones in afternoon and started him for Castle, working in garage putting connections on new piece of rubber hose for Bickle pump.

August 1922

August 1st - Hot, smoky, ashes falling - afternoon

West on Auto Road to Massive, working in garage on pump and staying around in case of fire, went to office and saw Woods re: letting survey party camp at Buffalo Park, went to Buffalo Park and told Brown.

August 2ⁿᵈ - Hot and smoky

To shack and saw Fuller and told him to go to Squaw Mountain and Cascade Trail, working on pump and on car no. 42 in afternoon, drove Mrs. Sibbald in evening.

August 4ᵗʰ - Hot and very smoky

Around garage fixing car no. 42 and up Sulphur Mountain for Sanson and pumps, went to Massive Lodge with spuds for Jones and patrol.

August 8ᵗʰ - Hot, smoky

Two trips to Bankhead with supplies and material for Clearwater, at garage and office, took bags to stable and shipped oats to Phillips and Ekstrom.

August 10ᵗʰ - Cloudy

Gathered up supplies for Ekstrom and took to Castle Mountain, to Squaw Mountain to get J.R. Warren to tell him of fire down Vermilion River, getting oil etc. for him to take, west to 5 mile board in evening, putting new carburetor on pump no. 2.

August 11ᵗʰ - Clear, no smoke

Repaired tire on car no. 10, went to Buffalo Park and took supplies to Warden Peyto, saw airplane circling around valley, very high, up for 30 minutes, took pump to river and tested same out and ran for 1 hour, shipped drills and hammer to Lake Louise.

August 12ᵗʰ - Rain afternoon and night

Cave Avenue, Sundance over to Healy Trail with pack for Warden E.W. Peyto, helped him pack same, about town after man for J.R. Warren, at garage in afternoon repairing top of car no. 15 and fixing headlights.

August 14ᵗʰ

Through Buffalo Park to dam, to office, stable and Zoo, took hay to Zoo for pony and buffalo, moved Fuller's outfit from shack to Buffalo Park, got car no. 15 ready for J.R. to go to Simpson River via Auto road to fire reported.

August 15ᵗʰ - Cloudy forenoon, rain afternoon

South up Spray River to Eau Claire camp after goat and brought to park, one old female had hurt hind leg and could

186

not travel so I shot her, fed horses at corral.

August 17ᵗʰ - Hot

To office and at garage and about town for Warren, went to see Harrison, to lower Buffalo Park hunting for meat horse and out towards dam and side of Cascade. Home on Tote Road and Auto Road.

August 18ᵗʰ - Hot

Lower buffalo pasture and hunted up horse and killed same and dressed carcass for Zoo - 5 hours, to Lake Minnewanka - helped unload boat from Vancouver (some lemon).

August 21ˢᵗ - Cloudy

To station with lumber and shipped to Lake Louise, to old intern camp after tin for Lake Louise cabin roof, getting paint etc. out for Phillips, filled up tank on car no. 42 and repairing same in afternoon, after supper drove same.

August 22ⁿᵈ - Windy

About town gathering up supplies and making up packs and fixing pack saddles, to rifle range with Dr. Fowler of Brooklyn and Dr. Atkin to try out rifles.

August 24ᵗʰ - Cloudy

Around garage, took back off car no. 42 (old no. 13), down to rifle range with Fred Hussey and wife, tested out their rifles.

August 25ᵗʰ - Fine

To Buffalo Park with oats for Fuller, west on Auto Road to 6 mile sand hill, crossed to track and shot horse with broken leg belonging to S. Ward - hit by train, shipped gasoline to Meredith, went back west, crossed to meadows and investigated two fires reported by Boyce, went to office and put in reports.

August 29ᵗʰ - Hot

To Loop and Golf Links chains and catching horses, saw airplane close over town and drop message for Chief Sibbald, to stable to see horse and turned out "Bud" - H.E. Sibbald's saddle horse, working on car no. 42.

August 31ˢᵗ - Cloudy, cool

To garage and Buffalo Park for sacks, got car no. 42 ready

for Parks Inspector, H.E. Sibbald to take Major Croile to Kootenay Park, took material to wardens' stores and checked off same, showed Warden Curren where I wanted shelves, helped fix up fender on car no. 10 (switches, protectors and masking tape).

September 1922
September 1st - Cloudy
At hospital all forenoon with boy undergoing operation, to Loop and Hot Springs in afternoon.
September 2nd - Fair, very strong wind at night
Around garage and office, fixed up shock absorber on car no 42, took Joe Woodworth to Bankhead and Anthracite on inspection trip - 5 hours.
September 5th - Fair
To Bankhead after pack saddles, about town gathering up outfit for H.E. Sibbald and Major Croile, took E.E. Stewart to Cave and Basin after money, getting saddles rigged up and helping Curren get outfit together for morning start to Spray Lakes, Major Croile looking for landing places for airplanes on patrol.
September 6th - Fine, west wind, cloudy toward evening
To pasture and Bretton Hall Hotel with Curren, helped him pack up and fix saddles for party (government) he had to take to Spray Lakes, to Lake Minnewanka with photographer and to Bankhead with hay for Wright and brought back man.
September 7th - Cloudy
To falls and CP Hotel, west on Auto Road to 2nd Lake and to Willow Creek and Echo River with Mr. Forrester, CNP publicity agent, crating and shipping pumping unit no. 6 (Mudge motor speeder) to Jasper Park, repaired shock absorbers on park inspector's car no. 42.
September 8th - Cloudy
To station and shipped brooms to Lake Louise, got out coal oil and gas for Warren to take to Kananaskis, Hot Springs, Golf Course and Sundance Canyon, about town, driving

Mr. Forrester to points of interest, at blacksmith shop helping repair pack saddle.

September 10th - Cloudy

Lower Road to Anthracite and back by Upper Road, picked up bear and lion skeletons, to Healy Trail and met Mr. Sibbald.

September 11th - Cloudy, showery

West on Auto Road and across to meadow, turned out "Heinie" and caught up "Goldie" my saddle horse - 5 hours, to park in afternoon and killed horse for Zoo - 4 hours, to office arranging for team to go after goat, 8 miles saddle horse, 5 miles car.

September 13th - Fine

West on Auto Road to Castle and south to Vermilion and Tokumm Creek with supplies for Oscar Ekstrom, took lumber and roofing to Bankhead on return.

September 14th - Fine

To Bankhead with lumber and roofing, putting battery and switch in car no. 42 for Mr. Sibbald, took Mr. Forrester to Lake Minnewanka, took grub to Bankhead for gang at Flints Park.

September 15th - Fine

To Bankhead, helped Wright pack up lumber for Flints Park, went to Johnston Canyon with Mr. Forrester taking pictures.

September 19th - Fine

West on Auto Road to Castle with Sanson's outfit, to office and about town, west on Auto Road to Lake Louise in afternoon, took paint to Pipestone Creek for McAulay and rope etc. to Phillips, home at 9:45 p.m.

September 21st - Fine, windy

Took HES to stable to see horse, to office, down to pasture and Zoo, saw caretaker re: fixing up polar bear's cage to be ready to receive new bear on arrival, west along hills north of Auto Road on high trails to 6 mile sand hill, did not see any sheep or deer on whole trip, back by road.

September 24th - Fine

Got call from Supt. at 1:30 that there was a fire 8 miles west on Auto Road between road and track, proceeded to 8 mile point with apparatus but could not locate any smoke or sign of fire, went west to near ten mile post, got on high point overlooking whole valley from Castle to Sawback but could not locate any smoke. I would surmise that someone had seen fishing parties' fire as there were two local cars parked near Sawback, intend to see these people, met JRW coming west and reported to him, 30 miles Bickle no. 10.

September 27th - Cloudy

Around town, to Buffalo Park, brought J.R. Warren back to town, to Camp Grounds to see Mumford and up west Auto Road - evening to 3rd Lake, saw nothing.

September 28th - Cloudy

To office and pasture, west on Auto Road with horses in afternoon, at fire near Whiskey Creek with J.R. Warren, using pumping unit no. 1 - 2 hours work, hobos' fire - 10 square yards - willow, sealed rifle for Carl Costello.

September 29th - Cloudy, windy

West on Auto Road to 7 mile board with Mr. Ross looking for pictures, got roofing etc. for Warren to take to Castle, to pasture and fed horses, fixing up car no. 42, cleaning plugs etc., to office, went to Squirrel Street to investigate fire, found kids playing with bonfire on road, made them get water and put out same.

September 30th - Cloudy

Went to Lake Louise with Mr. Ross locating good pictures and taking some of sheep on Auto Road.

October 1922

October 2nd - Cloudy

To office and garage, put oil and gas in car no. 42 for Warren, to pasture and got horses and took to upper meadow, got horse for Zoo and saddle horse to send to Lake Louise, west on Auto Road to 5 mile board, met Mr. Rungius near 3 mile board.

190

October 3rd - Fair

To pasture and fed horses, to office and garage, to Squaw Mountain Trail to see Mr. Hearle, to Loop and looking for break in wire and found same on Tunnel Mountain on Banff-Canmore line, 1 hour repairing, shipped supplies to Phillips, took Ekstrom's camp outfit to 7 mile spring.

October 6th - Fair

Crated pumping unit and shipped to Jasper to N.C. Sparks, towed Warren's car to garage, fixed up car no. 42 for him to go to Cochrane, Golf Links and built corral with P. Woodworth.

October 7th - Fine

Hauled up Mumford's camp outfit from Camp Grounds, at garage, put bolt in block of car no. 42, repaired radius rod on car no. 10, filled up both with gas, cutting lumber and making into packs at Crown yard, got a call at 6:30 p.m. re: horses in slough, went up with McAulay, McTrowe and Spencer and found two pack horses in centre of bog - almost covered - put in plank to get to same and pulled them out with team, home 9:45.

October 9th - Fine

To yard, west to meadows, caught up pack horse, about town gathering up outfit and supplies for Woodworth and J. Warren to take north, drove work horses from slough in meadows.

October 10th - Fine

To pasture and helped Woodworth pack horses, drove Warren to Buffalo Park, took load of lumber and rubberoid to Lake Minnewanka, went to Canmore Cabin after trail gang's outfit, got supplies from government stores and White's.

October 11th - Fine

To Bankhead and Lake Minnewanka, 2 trips with camp outfit for trail gang, to park after Mr. Wood and Phillips, west to 7 mile to see Ekstrom.

October 14th - Cloudy

To Golf Links and loaded sheep and sent to Buffalo Park,

posted diaries and gun seals to Macdonald at Radium Hot Springs, got out outfit for Curren, west on Auto Road to Sawback.

October 15th - Cloudy

To corral and fed horses, got call to fire west of Eldon, took Bickle and went west with J.R. Warren, met Wardens Phillips and Galvin at Eldon who said they had got section crews and stopped fire from crossing right of way.

October 16th - Fine

Took new army pack saddles to stores and checked out same, got Curren to box up those loaned by militia department.

October 18th - Fine

Working on building at Zoo turning it around, went to meadows and brought horses to town for Latam to take to winter range, numbered same.

October 19th - Fair

To Bankhead, 2 trips with supplies etc. for Latam, helped Latam pack horses for Red Deer, at office talking to Mr. Sibbald re: pumps and testing same, to Lake Minnewanka after men and outfit.

October 25th - Rain all day

To office and Auto Road to Squaw Mountain log chute to look for small deer reported killed, found remains of carcass - female fawn, been killed and eaten by coyotes, to Buffalo Park, to Hot Springs to sack coal, no coal there, to shack and field and wardens' stores, took saddles etc. to stores, got saddle horse shod.

October 26th - Rain and snow, cold and stormy on Sulphur Mountain

Packed coal to Observatory for N.B. Sanson with H. Fuller, changed forms on instrument for N.B. Sanson, made out list of tools etc. issued to G. Hislop for J.R. Warren and took same to office, put car no. 10 in garage.

October 29th - Fine

Banff to Kananaskis with work horses going to winter range, 28 miles rode.

October 30th - Cloudy
Kananaskis to Cameron's ranch near Morley, 20 miles rode, horses very little food and poor accommodation.

October 31st - Fine
Cameron's Ranch near Morley to Bottrel via Jackass Canyon and Grand Valley, about 30 miles rode, got word Warren's car had broken down and car would be out for us tomorrow.

November 1922
November 1st - Fine
At Bottrel taking shoes off horses with butcher knife and pincers - Warren arriving late with tools - 8 hours, left Bottrel for Banff 4:40, arrived Banff 11:30 p.m.

November 9th - Fine
Taking saddles etc. to store room from stable and checking up car no. 10, went to Castle and hauled lumber wall board to Massive, took stove to Massive and one to Castle for Ekstrom, saw E. Stenton coming down track on bicycle and after dark - could stand watching.

November 10th - Cloudy, cool
Banff to Morley and return - bringing home Warren's car, towed with Reo truck, 80 miles drove.

November 14th - Fine
Taking supplies and oil stove to Observatory for Sanson, took saddles etc. to Bankhead (car in poor condition).

November 15th - Fine, windy
Made 3 trips to Bankhead with supplies etc. for Wright and Fuller - left for Red Deer with pack horses, at corral hoof branding horses.

November 16th - Rain and sleet
West to Castle Mountain and south to Vermilion and Hawk Creek with outfit for Ekstrom, picked up highways truck driver, Brown, who had broken steering gear of Reo truck, snow very deep over summit - home 10:30.

November 17th - Fair
To Alpine Club House with Mr. Sibbald and engineer to

mark out sites and get levels for water tank, at garage taking down pumping units and checking up parts required for repairing.

November 18th - Fine

West to Massive Cabin and working on roof and ceiling of kitchen with Wardens Curren and J.R. Warren, putting beaver board on ceiling and rubberoid on roof, J.R. Warren drew my attention to paper in bell of phone, got word I would have to make trip to Weyburn, Sask.

November 20th - Fine

About town getting tools etc. ready and preparing for trip to Weyburn to bring back car used by Mr. Lloyd, left for Weyburn on train no. 2 at 10:30.

November 21st - Fine

Arrived at Weyburn, Sask at 9:30 p.m.

November 22nd - Fine

At Weyburn forenoon fixing up Ford car, left Weyburn at 11 a.m. for Milestone, 40 miles auto.

November 23rd - Fine

Milestone to Mortlach via Moose Jaw, 95 miles auto.

November 24th - Fine

Mortlach to Swift Current, 90 miles auto.

November 25th - Fine

Swift Current to Maple Creek, 98 miles auto.

November 26th - Fine

Maple Creek to Suffield, Alta, 95 miles auto.

November 27th - Cloudy

Suffield to Calgary, 175 miles auto.

November 28th - Snow, blizzard

Calgary to Cochrane to Kananaskis, 55 miles auto.

November 29th - Fair, cold

Kananaskis to Banff, 28 miles auto.

November 30th - Fine

To office and made out expense sheets, to Buffalo Park and got traps etc. and took to station for Ekstrom.

December 1922

December 1ˢᵗ - Fine

To office and garage, west to Mount Edith Pass and 3ʳᵈ Lake - testing phone with Mr. Sibbald, got wire from Golf Links and took to 3ʳᵈ Lake for sheep trap.

December 3ʳᵈ - Showery

To Station, Auto Road to Tote Road, down Tote Road and home along moose pasture fence to look at fire where Wards were burning rotten logs and brush on side of logging road.

December 4ᵗʰ - Cold, stormy, 30 below

Banff to Kananaskis with highways horses on way to Bottrel, 28 miles rode.

December 5ᵗʰ - Very cold, from east, 35 below

Kananaskis to Ghost River Ranch, 25 miles rode.

December 6ᵗʰ - Cold, stormy

Ghost River to Bottrel, pulled shoes off horses and came to Banff by car, 87 miles car, 25 miles rode.

December 9ᵗʰ - Cold, 25 below

To stables working on saddles with Naylor.

December 11ᵗʰ - Cold, 36 below

Took pack saddle to office, along Auto Road with E.W. Peyto gathering evergreen to make wreath for Mr. Vick.

December 12ᵗʰ - Cold, 30 below

At stables putting pack saddle together, at funeral of Mr. Vick, took hobbles and gun scabbard to office.

December 15ᵗʰ - Cold

Took remainder of saddles from stable to storeroom and got outfit and snowshoes for Naylor, Squaw Mountain to top of log chute and along Tote Road.

December 18ᵗʰ - Stormy

West on Auto Road to 2ⁿᵈ Lake, around town and outskirts looking for stray dogs, saw several fine male mule deer near graveyard and on side of Tunnel Mountain.

December 19ᵗʰ - Mild

Saw robin near sucker hole, west on Auto Road to 6 mile sand hill, set sheep trap at 3ʳᵈ Lake, to office, Squaw Mountain to logging camps, saw Pepper and Hislop on hill.

December 20th - Mild

West to sheep trap, had 2 sheep caught, came to town for truck, went back and took sheep to park, saw robin again, went west in afternoon and set trap, tame wolf out from movie cages, rode and car.

December 21st - Mild, cloudy

West on Auto Road to sheep trap and to station, at garage taking out Bickle and moving hose and bench to make room for radiator, out after Xmas trees for town - sent to Lux Theatre.

December 27th - Mild, some snow

Up Squaw Mountain on north side with Bill Peyto hunting mountain lion, found old kill, storm covered tracks till afternoon, ran onto hot tracks, not able to travel fast enough to keep up with dog, unable to make a kill, timber very thick and snow deep, impossible to do much with dogs in this piece of country, 10 miles walked, 9 hours.

Rosabelle Peyto and four of her children left to right:
Helen, Harold, Edith and Stan.

Banff Area Information

Alpine Club of Canada

In 1909/10 the Alpine Club of Canada built a club house and lodging rooms on the upper slope of Sulphur Mountain. This building contained a lounge area, and a dining hall. The building was demolished in 1974 after a new club house was built in Canmore in 1973. A. O. Wheeler, the first president of the Alpine Club of Canada, organized annual summer camps in various locations throughout the national parks.

Animal Paddocks or Buffalo Park

The animal paddocks were built in 1897 on both sides of the railway tracks, about 2 miles from Banff on the road towards Bankhead. Visitors could tour the area for free.

The native animals included elk, buffalo, moose, deer, mountain goats and mountain sheep. Non native animals such as yak and angora, Persian and four horned sheep were also kept here.

Anthracite

The town of Anthracite (6 km east of Banff) was a mining town started in 1886 soon after the CPR reached Banff. The Canadian Anthracite Company mined anthracite (a non-bituminous type of coal). Mr. H. W. McNeil (an American) operated the mine from 1891 till 1904. This mine closed about the same time as the Bankhead mines opened. Many of the residents left when the post office closed in 1905.

Frank Wheatley and his sons operated their own small mine from 1925 till 1950 when the government bought the land for the building of the Trans Canada Highway.

Banff CPR Station

The first train station was built in 1889 and used until its demolition in 1910. The second station was made from rough cut stucco and local rock. Kiosks were added to the ends of the building in the 1930's. When train travel to Banff was very popular many sightseeing tours started from the station. Tourists were also transported from the station to the town's hotels.

Banff Park Museum

The first museum opened in 1895 on the corner of Spray Avenue and Mountain Drive opposite the hospital. Mr. McLeod was appointed as the meteorologist and curator. When he died the following year, Norman B. Sanson was appointed.

In 1903 a new building opened on Banff Avenue on the north side of the bridge. This building is still in operation. The Moulton Park Hotel and Dance Pavilion were on this site prior to the museum.

Norman Sanson travelled extensively in the park for his studies of wildlife, geology and fauna. He also operated the observatory on Sulphur Mountain. Native artifacts he collected were given to Norman Luxton for display at the Luxton Museum.

Banff Springs CPR Hotel

The hotel first opened to visitors in 1888 with additions being constructed in 1904 and 1911. In 1926 the north wing was destroyed by fire. Reconstruction was completed the following year. It was not until 1969 that the hotel began to stay open year round.

Banff Zoo and Aviary

The Aviary opened in 1904 on the grounds behind the Banff Park Museum with eight pheasants donated by CPR Vice President William Whyte. Later pools were added for geese, ducks and coots. Cages for the Zoo were finished in 1908. The animals included bears, fox, wolves, coyotes, lynx, mountain lions, badgers, martens, marmots and birds such as hawks, eagles and owls. Non native species included monkeys and polar bears. At one time the Zoo had about 60 animals. By the late 1920's and the early 1930's, visitors

198

were being encouraged to view more of the animals in the wild. The Zoo closed in 1937 and the cages were dismantled. Some of the animals were returned to the wild and others shipped to the Calgary Zoo.

Bankhead

This coal mining town was built in 1904 by the Canadian Pacific Railway along the road to Lake Minnewanka. The town was named by Lord Strathcona in 1905 after Bankhead in the county of Banffshire, Scotland. From 1904 until the mines closed in 1923, the town flourished with a population of over 900. However, a reduced demand for coal and a miners' strike closed the mines. The town had a municipal water supply, sewage system and electric power before either Banff or Canmore.

The anthracite coal was mined from Cascade Mountain. A railway spur line took the coal 3 km to the main CPR line at Bankhead Station (some 4 km east of the Banff Station). The old Bankhead Station is now located near the Banff Hostel on Tunnel Mountain Road.

Many of the buildings were moved to Banff and Canmore. The church was moved to the Forest Lawn area of Calgary. A self guided trail leads past the old mine building ruins.

Bow River Bridge

The present day bridge was constructed in 1923 to replace the old steel bridge which was moved downstream during the construction of the present bridge. The native head carvings on the sides of the bridge are the work of a Calgary sculptor named Thompson.

Brett Sanitarium

This was one of the first two hotels in Banff. Dr. Brett's building was located on the south side of the bridge where the present day Administrative Building and Cascades of Time Gardens are now located. The building served as both a hotel and a hospital. An opera house was added in 1904 and used for various social functions. The name changed over the years from Brett Sanitarium Hotel to Sanitarium Hotel and finally Bretton Hall Hotel.

Camp Grounds

The first camp ground in the Banff area opened in 1923 near the confluence of the Bow and Spray Rivers below the Banff Springs Hotel. This helped to reduce the problems of fire and litter caused by motorists camping randomly. In 1928 the camp ground was moved to the present location of the Tunnel Mountain campground.

Canmore

The town of Canmore is about 17 km south east of Banff. The CPR set up the first divisional point west of Calgary in this area in 1884. The name was probably selected by Donald A. Smith of the CPR in honour of King Malcolm III from Canmore, Scotland (king of the Scots from 1057 to 1093).

Cave and Basin

The Cave and Basin was discovered in 1885 by three railway workers, William McCardell, Thomas McCardell, and Frank McCabe. Before the tunnel was built to reach the Cave in 1886, visitors had to descend a ladder through a hole in the roof of the cave. The architect Walter Painter designed the structure around the main pool area (built 1912-14). Painter also designed the centre block of the Banff Springs Hotel and Chateau Lake Louise. Behind the main structure of the Cave and Basin is the pool area used prior to 1914.

In 1985 the complex was enlarged to recognize the Canadian National Parks Centennial with a museum being added on the second level. The refurbished pool operated from 1985 to 1993 when it again closed due to maintenance problems.

Duthil

A few people lived in this area near the locally named "seven mile hill" east of Banff on the north side of the Trans Canada Highway. A small fish hatchery also operated in the area for a few years. It was named after Duthil, Inverness, Scotland.

Fish Hatchery

The fish hatchery opened in 1914 between Glen Avenue and Bow Falls. The building (54 feet by 31 feet) had a capacity of three million fish. Superintendent R. T. Rodd lived in the nearby residence.

By 1916 there were four outdoor pools with holding troughs located at Spray Lakes. In 1931 the Department of the Interior (Parks Canada) assumed control and expanded the stocking program.

The hatchery closed in 1956 and operations were moved to Duthil. Two old POW (prisoner of war) buildings were joined together to accommodate twelve spring fed hatching troughs. Later operations moved to the Anthracite area using water from Johnson Lake. By the late 1960's fish hatchery operations in the Banff area had ceased.

Garbage Grounds

In the journals the names Garbage Dump and Nuisance Grounds are also used. The Garbage Grounds at this time were across the Spray River Bridge along the Loop Drive near the Golf Course.

Golf Course or Golf Links

A nine hole course beside the Loop Drive was opened in 1911 by the CPR. When the camp ground moved from the area near the confluence of the Bow and Spray Rivers, the course was enlarged to eighteen holes.

Internment Camp

On the Bow Valley Parkway west of Banff, there is a memorial to the men who were interned at this camp near the base of Castle Mountain during World War I. The men (eastern Europeans) were considered aliens by the Canadian government.

The men were put to work on projects such as the construction of the Banff-Lake Louise road and the Banff-Vermilion Pass road. They also worked on various other projects throughout the park. During the winter they were moved to a camp near the Cave and Basin and put to work on projects such as cutting trees and clearing brush from road allowances.

Johnston Canyon

The canyon is on the Bow Valley Parkway about 18 km west of the junction with the Trans Canada Highway. Construction of the trail along the canyon was started in 1917. In 1920 the first visitor facilities were added.

Loop Drive

This road goes across the Spray River Bridge below the Banff Springs Hotel. The Golf Course and Garbage Grounds were along the road.

Mather's boat house

In 1888 Mr. J. Ryan started a canoe and launch (Mountain Belle) operation on the Bow River. William Mather took over the operation in the late 1890's. By 1904 he had added more canoes and rowboats as well as a new motor launch.

Minnewanka, Lake

Lake Minnewanka is located north east of Banff. It is the largest lake in Canada's mountain national parks. In 1841 George Simpson of the Hudson's Bay Company became the first non-native man to view the lake. In 1888 the Department of the Interior named the lake "Minnewanka" or "lake of the water spirit". Some of the other names have been Devil's Lake, Cannibal Lake, Peechee Lake, and Long Lake.

In 1886 Walter Astley built a chalet named the Beach House which operated until 1912. In 1899 the CPR built a 200 foot pier and started a launch operation. Norman Luxton operated a chalet on the south shore from the early 1900's until 1912. This chalet and the Beach House did not survive the raising of the water level 3.5 metres when a Calgary Power storage dam was constructed in 1912. Many of the summer cottages were moved to higher ground.

When the second dam was added slightly downstream from the first dam in 1942, the water level rose another 20 metres. The buildings of the Minnewanka Landing settlement were either moved, torn down or just covered when the water level rose.

Today a concession and a tour boat business is a reminder of the early days.

Moffatt's Dairy

The dairy was located on the far side of the railway tracks just past the railway station at the west entrance to Banff.

Moulton Park Hotel

This early Banff hotel was located in the park area behind the Banff Park Museum. It was built of logs floated downstream from the demolition of old buildings at Silver City (a short lived boom town along the present day Bow Valley Parkway). A dance hall was added to the hotel about 1888 or 1889.

Park Roads

In 1909 work was started on a road between Calgary and Banff. The road was completed in 1911. By 1914 motorists were allowed on Banff Avenue and as far as the Banff Springs Hotel. Cars were allowed on Lynx and Caribou Streets in 1915. Speed limits were 8 mph in town, 4 mph at road crossings, and 15 mph out of town.

In 1917 roads were oiled rather than watered to lay the dust. Speed limits were increased in 1919 to 15 mph in town, 8 mph at crossings, and 25 mph out of town.

By 1921 it was possible to drive to Lake Louise. The Banff-Windermere Road was officially opened in 1923. It was possible to drive to Field and Golden by 1927. The Icefields Parkway (Lake Louise to Jasper) opened in 1940.

Recreation Grounds

A large swampy area adjacent to the Bow River and accessible from Cave Avenue was drained in 1915 for the development of the Recreation Grounds. Architect Frank Lloyd Wright, assisted by F.C. Sullivan, was hired to build a pavilion with stoves and fireplaces. Other facilities included tennis courts and a playground. Visitors could walk or drive along Cave Avenue, or use the motor launch, a canoe or rowboat to reach the grounds. The pavilion was demolished after World War II and replaced with cooking shelters, tables, benches and barbeque pits.

Siding 29

When the CPR tracks first reached the Banff area in 1883, a station and a section house were built near where the present day highway leading east out of Banff passes under the railway tracks. Some people did live in this area but the settlement was short lived. With the opening of the Banff Station, Siding 29 became only a memory by 1897.

Sulphur Mountain and Observatory

Work began on a bridle trail up the mountain in 1902. The observatory (about 7500 feet) was finished in 1903. This stone building (14 feet by 15 feet) had an observation tower 26 feet high. Measurements could be taken on wind velocity and currents, and temperatures.

Norman Sanson travelled up to the observatory weekly, summer and winter, to check the equipment and change the recording sheets. He was honoured in 1931 when many friends joined him at the observatory for a sunrise breakfast on the occasion of his 1000th ascent. His last climb was about 1945 at the age of 83. In 1948 the peak on which the observatory is located was named Sanson Peak.

Tote Road

This road led from the Animal Paddocks or Buffalo Park near the present day warden headquarters over to the road leading west out of Banff near the access road to Mount Norquay.

Upper Hot Springs

In 1886 two bath houses were built near the Upper Hot Springs by Dr. R.G. Brett and by Whitman McNulty. Water was also pumped to the Banff Springs Hotel and the Brett Sanitarium Hotel.

When Dr. Brett's Grand View Villa Hotel near the Hot Springs burned in 1901, the government decided to take over the management of the Hot Springs and constructed a bath house, a pool and a caretaker's house. In 1996 the present day facility reopened after extensive renovations.

Water and Power

Electric power lines from Bankhead to Banff were built in 1904/05. A power house was built in 1924 to supply all of Banff with electricity. Calgary Power took over this operation in 1942.

Water mains and sewer lines were constructed in Banff in 1905/06 with Forty Mile Creek being the town's first water source.

Car on Lake Minnewanka Road. Whyte Museum of the
Canadian Rockies. V263 NA71-4334.

Walter Peyto and Howard Sibbald with fire pump. Whyte
Museum of the Canadian Rockies. V573 NA66-2179.

Biographies for 1914 to 1922

Malcolm Amoss - The "Wrigley's Alberta Directory" (1920) lists an N.E. Amoss as a mechanic foreman with Brewster Transport Co. Ltd. This may be the same person.

Charlie Archibald - He came west to Calgary from Badeck, N.S. in 1907. After moving to Banff in 1912, he spend four years overseas in World War I. He worked on maintenance after the war and in 1924 entered the government electrical service. Charlie died at age fifty one in either 1938 or 1939.

Mrs. Ashton - She was the wife of Dr. Bevan Ashton. She was born in Copenhagen, Denmark and came to Canada in 1893. Before settling in Banff, she had lived in Winnipeg, Regina and Moose Jaw. She died in 1943 at the age of sixty nine.

Dr. Bevan Ashton (1872-1940) - The very popular Dr. Ashton came from England. In 1911 he and his wife bought the Upper Hot Springs from the Thomson Brothers and operated the facility under the name of Upper Hot Springs Hotel. His studies were in osteopathy.

Dr. Gilbert M. Atkin (1877-1969) - He moved to Banff from Ontario in 1910 and established the Atkin Clinic which operated for over fifty years. During World War I, the doctor served overseas as a captain in the Army Medical Corps. He was also very active in community activities. His wife was Eva M. (1884-1968).

Fred Ballard - He first came to Banff in 1901. Fred was a member of several important climbing parties including Sir James Outram's first ascent of Mount Columbia in 1902 and an expedition that same year when Professsor J. Norman Collie joined Outram to make the first ascent of

Mount Forbes. Fred's early business ventures in Banff included a photographic studio and a laundry. He also contracted for house building. He died in 1945 at the age of seventy seven.

Jack Ballard - He resided in the Banff area prior to the beginning of the century until 1915. Jack was known as an outstanding guide and packer. He was in his late seventies when he died in Florida in 1956.

Jack Bevan - He served as a warden in Rocky Mountains Park (later Banff) in 1913 and from 1914 to 1917. Jack also worked for Brewster Transport and had organized field trips.

Karl H. Bingay - He was a native of Yarmouth, N.S. In 1915 Karl joined the 10th Battalion. After being wounded in one lung he was invalided home in 1916. He came to the Banff area about 1920 and worked as a plumbing inspector and as a clerk for the Department of the Interior. He died in 1937 at the age of fifty seven.

Joe Blair - He worked as a chef at the Mount Royal Hotel and later was the proprietor of the Club Café. He also sponsored a hockey team.

James (Jim) Boyce - Jim arrived in Banff in 1911 to work as a trail builder. Later he became a mountain guide and cook. He first worked as a guide for Jimmy Simpson before starting his own outfitting business with Max Brooks. One of his clients was the artist, Carl Rungius. Another of his clients was Caroline Hinman in the 1920s. Jim helped build various lodges in the Lake Louise area and at one time ran Skoki Lodge. He also worked on the construction of cabins on the Icefields Parkway. He died in 1982 at the age of ninety.

Joe Boyce - Joe came west from New Brunswick and spent several years following mineral and timber prospects in the United States and British Columbia before coming to Banff. Joe spent many years as a trail maker for the government. He died at the age of seventy one. His wife was Wilhelmina (1866-1952).

Dr. Harry Brett (1879-1925) - Dr. Brett was born in Ontario, the son of Dr. Robert G. Brett. He received his education from St. John's, Winnipeg and the Manitoba Medical College. After post graduate work in New York and at Mayo Brothers, Rochester, Minnesota, he spent a year in London and Vienna. He worked with his father at the Brett Sanitarium in Banff and also with Dr. Gilbert Atkin. The Sanitarium Hotel later became known as the Bretton Hall Hotel.

Dr. Robert G. Brett (1851-1929) - Dr. Brett first came west from Ontario in the early 1870s as a surveyor for the CPR. When he settled in Banff after the completion of the railway, he developed the Sanitarium Hotel (a combined hospital and hotel) at the south end of Banff Avenue in the area now occupied by the Administration Building. He and his son developed the Grand View Villa adjacent to the Upper Hot Springs, the Sanitarium Bottling Works and the Brett Block on Banff Avenue. Dr. Brett was a member of the Legislative Assembly of the North West Territories from 1888 to 1901. He was appointed Alberta's second Lieutenant Governor from 1915 to 1925. His wife Louise died in 1935.

Mrs. Helen Brett - She was born in New Brunswick. While journeying west towards Vancouver in 1906 she stopped off in Banff and began work at the Brett Sanitarium Hospital. In 1912 she married Dr. Harry Brett. Helen assisted her husband and father-in-law with the running of the hospital. After her husband's death in 1925, Helen remained a Banff resident until her death in 1965 at the age of eighty eight.

Bill Brewster (1880-1970) - He was born in Orillia, Ontario and came to Banff with his family in 1887. In 1896 Bill went north for the Klondike Gold Rush. After returning to Banff, he went into business with his brother Jim. Bill then travelled to South America managing ranges in Argentina and Ecuador before heading north to Mexico and Texas. He and a partner set up a sightseeing business in Glacier Park, Montana. When he retired he returned to Banff.

Jim Brewster (1882-1947) - He came to Banff in 1887 with his family. By 1900, Jim and his brother Bill (with their father's support) had established W. and J. Brewster, Guides and Packers. The name changed to Brewster Brothers in 1904 with the investment by Phil Moore and Fred Hussey. The company expanded quickly to include a livery stable, a general store, an opera house, the Mount Royal Hotel and the rights to the CPR livery operations. As the company developed under the name of Brewster Transport, it acquired a set of open touring cars and by the 1920s operated the first White buses in the park.

John Brewster (1852-1941) - In 1887 he came to Banff with his young family from Kingston, Ontario. John started a dairy at the corner of Banff Avenue and Moose Street. In 1896 he moved the dairy across the tracks just beyond the train station. He sold the dairy business to Frank Wellman, who in turn sold it to Charles Moffatt in 1911.

F.O. (Pat) Brewster (1896-1982) - Pat worked as a trail guide, outfitter and businessman. After World War I service, he established the first permanent camp for the CPR at Lake O'Hara. In 1926 Pat took over Brewster Transport from his brothers Jim and Bill. In the 1930s he became involved with skiing at Assiniboine, Skoki and Sunshine.

Between 1975 and 1982 he wrote three books about the Banff area.

Ike Brooks - He came to Banff in 1911 and worked for Brewster Co. looking after horses. In 1921 he moved to Sundre to start a ranch of his own. He was seventy five at the time of his passing in California in 1959.

J.M. Brooks - He was a seasonal warden in the Banff area in 1917.

Belmore Browne - This New York native came to Banff in 1920 at the age of forty. He became widely known as an explorer and naturalist. He first lived in the cabin that was the town's first museum at 124 Spray Avenue. He later added a studio and house (it became known as Elkhorn Lodge). Browne devoted much of his time to painting in the mountains, fishing and hunting. He died in 1954.

Howard Caine - He worked as a warden in Banff National Park from 1913 to 1917.

Alf Capel - He came to Banff from Cheshire, England in 1910. After service in World War I, he was employed by the Dominion Government until his retirement in 1954. He died at the age of sixty nine in 1958.

Billy Carver - Billy was known to local residents as The Hermit. He had come to Canada from St. John's Wood, London, England in about 1908. He lived for many years in a small cabin near Johnson Lake. In the summers he travelled north to the Brazeau area mines. He had very little contact with Banff area residents except a Chinese market gardener near Anthracite. He was also known by the names of Billy Reader and Billy Phillips. In late 1937 two local boys stopped by the cabin and found Billy to be very sick. Walter Peyto helped to bring him to the hospital. However

Billy's health remained poor and he died soon after in Gleichen. His cabin has an historic plaque.

Child - There were four brothers in this family (George, William, John and Walter). George died in Vancouver in 1940. Walter served as a temporary warden in Banff in 1929 and from 1939 to 1944. William helped rescue Mrs. Stone and her husband's body from Mount Eon in 1921.

Cyril Childe - He was an engineer for the Department of the Interior, Parks Branch. In World War I he served with the 1st Division Cyclists. After the war he was active with Legion and militia activities. He died in 1973.

S.J. Clarke (1852-1918) - He was born in Huntingdon, Quebec. He was a member of the RNWMP from 1876 till 1882 when he left and settled in Calgary. After serving as an alderman and commissioner he moved to Banff and was Superintendent of the park from 1912 to 1918.

Barney Collison - He came west from Iroquois, Ontario in 1905, although he soon returned east due to a family illness. When he returned west, he began his legal practice in Calgary with the famous Paddy Nolan. Collison was appointed to the position of commissioner of the Dominion Park police and park magistrate in 1916 and moved to Banff. He is credited with helping organize the first Banff Winter Carnival in February, 1917. He died in Calgary at the age of seventy three.

W.W. Cory - He was born in Strathroy, Ontario. He was Deputy Minister of the Interior and made several visits to Banff. His sons Lou and Wilf accompanied him on at least one visit.

Major Croile - In 1920 he was in charge of the air forestry patrol at Morley. By 1922 he was working at the High

River airport.

Lou Crosby (1887-1964) - A native of Prince Edward Island, Lou moved west, arriving in Calgary in 1907. He began his fifty seven year career with Brewster Transport as a bookkeeper and rose to the position of chairman of the company. His interests included serving on the school board for thirty years, working on the winter carnival, and climbing and hiking. He was also an active member of the Alpine Club of Canada.

John Curren Jr. - He emigrated from Scotland in 1887 as a small boy and lived in Anthracite and Banff. His father, John Donaldson Curren (1852-1940), worked in the Georgetown mine near Canmore starting in 1885 and later worked at the Anthracite mine. John Jr. was well known by many climbers, hikers, trail riders and tourists during his twenty five years as a warden starting in 1916. In 1941 he moved to Vancouver. He died in 1953. His sister Annie married Dave White, Sr.

John M. Dignall (1888-1956) - This native of Wales arrived in Banff in 1913. For thirty seven years he worked as chief clerk accountant with the Dominion Government in Banff and Field. His wife was Eva (1890-1974).

Mrs. Nora(h) Drummond Davis - She was a painter of big game animals who arrived in the Banff area about 1920. Her home was a log cabin on the lower slopes of Mount Norquay where today's access road starts. She lived there for eight or nine years with her cats, Airedale dogs and horse. Her husband came to visit from England but returned home after about a year. Her studio burned down about 1927 and Mrs. Drummond Davis moved on to Victoria where she died in 1950.

Hugh Dyer - He came from Suffolk, England in 1886.

Hugh arrived in Bankhead in 1905 where he operated the Bankhead Dairy. He moved to Banff about 1918 and was seventy nine at the time of his passing in 1961.

James T. Edwards (1884 or 1885-1971) - He came to Bankhead from Stonehaven, Scotland in 1906 and began working at Brewster's stables. He later operated his own taxi business for a number of years and then worked for Unwin's lumber yard from 1924 to 1954. His wife was Jeanie (1892-1964).

John Edwards - He moved from Shropshire, England to Banff in 1911. He was employed by the Parks Department for twenty five years as a wheelwright.

Ralph Edwards - Ralph came to Canada in 1888 from Kent, England. In 1894 he joined Tom Wilson as a guide and packer. He also made several trips with Bill and Jim Brewster. In 1940 he was made head of the Government Information Bureau in Banff. Among his many accomplishments was the book "Trail to the Charmed Land" on the early days in the park. He was ninety when he passed away in 1959.

Oscar Ekstrom - Oscar died from suffocation in 1926 when his truck rolled on the Banff-Lake Louise road about two miles west of Banff. At the time of his death, he was the Game and Fire Warden in the Marble Canyon area.

Ben Fay - He was born in Mendota, Illinois. Ben and his wife moved to Bankhead in 1905 where they lived until moving to Rocky Mountain House in 1920. He was seventy two at the time of his passing in 1954.

James and Mrs. Fee - He worked as a caretaker at the Zoo.

Forbes Finlayson - He was born in Ontario. He lived the

last twenty years of his life in Victoria although he returned to Banff each summer to help his son, Jack, operate the Shell Oil Service Station. He died in Victoria in 1948 at the age of sixty five.

George "Ockey" Fowles - He operated the Anthracite Dairy and also ran the Hub Pool Room and Lux Theatre. George was an ardent hockey fan and supporter of the Winter Carnival. He was also interested in whippet racing. In 1937 he died in Victoria. His brother-in-law was Alf Capel.

Burton S. Fox (1862-1951) - This native of Stockport, Ontario spent twenty nine years in Banff. He was manager of the fish hatchery.

Thomas Frayne (1887-1974) - Thomas came to Canada in 1907 from Cheshire, England arriving in the Banff area in 1911. One of his early jobs was driving a team for Dr. Brett. He also helped make the native faces on the sides of the Bow River Bridge. In 1920 he joined Jimmy Simpson as a guide and trail cook. Later he joined the parks department. One of his main jobs was foreman of the "Mosquito Gang" in the summer dealing with the control of mosquitoes around Banff.

Cyril Fuller - A native of Cambridge, England, Fuller arrived in Canada in 1898 and settled with his family near Innisfail. He served in both the Boer War and World War I. In 1921 he joined the wardens and served for twenty seven years. He died in 1973 at the age of ninety one.

Harold Fuller (1895-1976) - Harold came to Banff in 1909 to join his brother Cyril. In World War I he served with the 50th Battalion in France and was twice wounded. He served as a park warden from 1921 to 1934 working in areas such as Massive, Bankhead, Lake Louise and Marble Canyon.

He also helped build numerous bridges and cabins. In addition he helped with the building of the Cascades of Time Garden around the Administration Building at the south end of Banff Avenue.

Walter Fulmer - He came to Banff in 1887 as a Dominion Land Surveyor under the supervision of Andrew St. Cyr. He later started his own business which included a stable of horses, a draying business, baggage and transfer services. He also had timber rights behind Sundance Canyon.

William Furnell - He came west from Ontario in 1904. For years he was in charge of the Bankhead and Banff Electric Plant and Lighting. He moved to Vancouver in 1924 due to ill health and died three years later at the age of fifty five.

William George Fyfe (1878-1968) - Fyfe came to Canada in the 1890s from Cullen, Banffshire, Scotland. He had a guide and outfitting business before joining the parks department as the first warden at Castle Mountain. He held a number of government positions prior to his retirement in 1945. In 1916 he was accidentally shot by a guard at the Castle Mountain Internment Camp. His sister, Nellie McGregor, married Reggie Holmes who died in 1919. Her second husband was Arthur Unwin. Fyfe's father, W.H. Fyfe, also lived in the Banff area about this same time. His father died in 1917.

George Gallop - He died in 1929 during an appendicitis operation. He had lived in Banff for a number of years but had returned to England in 1921. His brother William lived in Banff.

Dan F. Galvin - D.F. Galvin served as a warden in the Banff area from 1926 to 1929.

Walter Garrett - A native of Hampshire, England, Walter

came to Alberta about 1890 and worked on CPR construction with Dave White, a pioneer Banff resident. Walter took up residence in Banff in 1905 and worked in various government positions, retiring in 1930 from his position in charge of the Upper Hot Springs Bath House. He died in 1942.

Hugh Gordon - He was born at Wellington Villa, Nairn, Scotland in 1873. He and his brother came to the Columbia Valley in B.C. in 1890 to work at sheep ranching and freighting. He had managed the Queen's Hotel in Golden and the Victoria Hotel in Calgary before becoming the manager of Banff's King Edward Hotel. His other business interests included a confectionary and ice cream parlour, and the Cave and Basin Tea Room which burned in 1933. Health problems forced him to temporarily leave Banff in 1932. On his return he became police magistrate for awhile and also worked for the government at the Cave and Basin before leaving Banff a second time due to illness. He died in 1948.

Captain Grey - He came to Banff in 1913 as chief engineer of roads. After four years away during World War I, he returned to the same position. In 1920 J.M. Wardle replaced him.

Charley Griffith - He was on the CPR depot staff.

William H. Griffith - This native of Worchestershire, England resided in the area between Canmore and Lake Louise for forty eight years. He worked as section foreman at Castle Mountain for eight years and then for the Anthracite and Canmore Coal Companies for thirty eight years. He worked as temporary warden in 1921. He died in Canmore in 1932 at the age of seventy two.

J.B. Harkin - He was commissioner of Dominion Parks

during the early part of the 20th Century. He died in 1955 just two days short of his eightieth birthday.

Byron Harmon (1875-1942) - This native of Tacoma, Washington was a resident of Banff for thirty nine years. He was an enthusiastic mountain climber who became well known for his outstanding collection of mountain photographs. For nineteen years, Byron operated a photographic business in Banff which later expanded to include a drugstore (Harmony Drugs) and then a café in connection with the store. For some years he was an official photographer for the CPR. He died in Canmore.

George Harrison (d. 1968) - He was one of the four original guides who worked with the Brewster brothers (Jim and Bill). The others were Bert Sibbald, Frank Wellman and Bob Logan. George came to Banff in 1903 from Iowa. He later operated his own outfitting and guiding business before working for the government in Banff until his retirement.

E. Hearle - He was well known for the number of years he came west from Ottawa to organize the mosquito control operations around Banff.

Lou Hill - He served as a park warden in 1913. Later he became fire chief in Banff.

Ben Holbrow - He came from England during construction of the CPR. He then worked in the first saw mill at Kananaskis run by Colonel James Walker of Calgary. Later he cut and sold timber in and around Banff.

Reggie Holmes - He was born in Staines, England. When he first came to Canada he had a short lived outfitting business with Elliott Barnes, the photographer. He was part of Mary Schaffer's 1908 expedition to Maligne Lake with Billy Warren and Sid Unwin. Health problems forced him off the trail about 1914 and he worked for a short time as the government timekeeper at the Park Museum. He lived in Vancouver from 1915 to 1917 before returning to Banff. He died in 1919. His widow married Arthur Unwin.

Steve Hope - He came from England in 1913 and resided in Banff for 53 years until his death at the age of seventy nine. He worked as a blacksmith.

J.L. Horsfall - He worked as an accountant for the Department of the Interior, Parks Branch.

Fred Hussey - He first came to Banff from the USA in 1900. In 1904 he and Phil Moore entered into partnership in the Brewster Transport Co. with Jim and Bill Brewster. He lived in the elegant bachelor dwelling at the corner of Moose Street and Banff Avenue. The building was later known as the Brewster Bungalow and then as Mile Hi Lodge. He died in 1930.

Jack James - He served as game warden at the ranger station just west of Canmore, retiring in 1938 and moving to Banff. He died in 1943.

Gus Johnson - He was born in Norway and came to Banff in 1912. He became a strong promoter of ski jumping. He died in 1927.

Gus Johnson - the second person named Gus Johnson was a section foreman for the CPR.

Robert H. (Casey) Jones - He came from England after the turn of the century and worked as a carpenter until his retirement. He died in 1977 at the age of ninety.

Art Jordan - He was a Brewster employee who later moved to Calgary to work for the CPR.

Archibald Keith - He was from Somerset, England. After arriving in Banff in 1913, he worked as a carpenter at the Banff Springs Hotel. Later he worked as a federal government teamster and truck driver before returning to carpentry. He died in 1971 at the age of eighty eight.

Ulysses La Casse (1888-1972) - La Casse came west from Seaforth, Ontario to Medicine Hat at the age of sixteen and first worked as a baker. He first settled in the Banff area in 1908 and spent some time guiding before working as a trail foreman and later joining the warden service. As a warden he worked in the districts of Saskatchewan River, Pipestone and Lake Louise, and Castle Mountain where he spent ten years. He retired in 1949.

Dr. James Lafferty (1853-1921) - He was born in Ontario. Dr. Lafferty had practised medicine in Ontario before working in Winnipeg from 1881 to 1885. He then moved on to Calgary. He became the Chief Surgeon for the CPR and was the first president of the Alberta College of Physicians and Surgeons. He also established and operated a system of private banks from Winnipeg to the west coast.

John Wesley Latam - Born in Leduc, Alberta, he was well known in the Banff and Canmore area. He worked as a warden in Banff National Park. He also worked at the government ranch. For the last ten years of his life, he was the public works foreman for the village of Canmore. He died in 1946 at the age of fifty three, just two days after a fall from his horse.

Art Latimer - He came to Canmore in 1903 from Metcalfe, Ontario and became manager of the Rundle Mountain Trading Company in 1911. He held this position until his passing in 1945.

Henry (Harry) Leacock (1874-1956) - He came to Banff in 1908 from England. He worked as a storekeeper and later as the Banff Park treasurer until his retirement. He served in both the Boer War and World War I.

Sir James Lougheed - This Calgary lawyer had a family home in Banff. He married the daughter of Richard Hardisty (Chief Factor of Fort Edmonton). In 1911 he was appointed to the Borden federal cabinet as Minister without Portfolio. His grandson, Peter Lougheed, became Premier of Alberta.

Oscar Lovgren - He was the young Swedish labourer killed by a grizzly bear near Spray Lakes in October, 1914.

George Luxton - He travelled to Banff from Minnesota for the summers and helped operate the Lux Theatre from 1913 to 1915. He passed away in Minnesota in 1962 at the age of eighty, one month after his brother Norman's death. Norman operated the Luxton Museum and Lux Theatre. He was also a former editor of The Banff Crag and Canyon.

John MacKay (1846-1934) - He came west from Pictou County, Nova Scotia. He worked in mines in Nanaimo, B.C., Anthracite, Canmore, Cochrane and Bankhead. He helped build a trail north from Laggan (Lake Louise) to the North Saskatchewan River past Bow Lake in 1911. After the Bankhead mine closed in 1923, John was employed by the Engineering Department of Rocky Mountains Park (later Banff National Park).

William Mather - He came to Ontario from Scotland with his family in 1883. William worked as timekeeper for the Eau Claire Lumber Co. while operating a general store in Anthracite. After moving to Banff, he opened up a boat business on the Bow River. He was also very interested in winter sports. His son Allen later operated the skating rink. Allen married Ruth Carpenter, a niece of Mary Schaffer

Warren. William died in 1927.

Charles H. McAulay (1874-1966) - McAulay came to Bankhead in 1907 from Truro, Nova Scotia. After being in charge of the briquette plant until 1912, he was appointed general construction foreman for Rocky Mountains Park until his retirement from park service in 1939. He then became foreman with the Mannix Construction Company and Calgary Power, working on projects at Lake Minnewanka, Kananaskis Lakes and Spray Lakes. His wife was Cecilia (1889-1953).

John McCormick - He came to Canada from Ireland at the age of eighteen. By 1903 he had settled in the Banff area and became foreman of the Brett Stables. He remained as the foreman when the Bretton Hall and King Edward Hotel Stables combined. As the use of cars increased, he went into the taxi business.

James McLeod (1878-1955) - He was a Banff businessman who first worked in the Lake Louise area in 1906. From 1911 to 1920 he was a manager for Brewster Transport Co. In 1921 he founded Rocky Mountain Tours and Transport Co. with William Warren. It amalgamated with Brewster Transport in 1957. In 1945 he and Earl Gammon bought Ye Olde Homestead Hotel.

Douglas K. McTrowe - He was born in Inverness, Scotland. When he came to Canada in 1889 he first settled in Kitchener, Ontario before moving on to Banff in 1902. He was employed by Jim Brewster and later became barn boss at the old government stables. He was caretaker at the Buffalo Paddock from 1922 until his retirement. He died in 1950 at the age of seventy two. Walter Peyto was one of his pallbearers.

J.J. Meredith - He spent twenty seven years in the warden service in the Radium area serving as the chief park warden for Kootenay National Park from 1937 to 1949.

William L. (Bill) Mitcheltree (1877-1938) - The Ontario native had operated meat markets in Vernon and Revelstoke before coming to Banff in 1917. He owned the Banff Meat Market and also worked as a fishing guide for the Banff Springs Hotel. In 1938 he drowned in the Bow River west of Banff. Walter Peyto was the one who located the body. Bill's wife was Edith (1876-1957).

Charles Moffatt - He came to Banff from Maple Creek, Saskatchewan in 1910. In 1911 he purchased the dairy business of Frank Wellman. This dairy was started by John Brewster at the corner of Banff Avenue and Moose Street and later moved across the tracks just beyond the CPR Banff Station in 1896. When fire destroyed the barn in 1938, Moffatt sold his cows and milk route to the Union Milk Co. He died in 1940 at the age of seventy one. Some sources spell his name "Moffat".

Phil Moore (1880-1951) **and Pearl Brewster Moore** (1889-1973) - In 1902 Phil Moore and his Princeton friend, Fred Hussey, attended the New York Sportsman Show. They talked with Jim and Bill Brewster and were convinced to journey to Banff for a hunting trip. This resulted in both young Americans moving to Banff and investing in the Brewster Brothers business. In 1907 Phil married Pearl Brewster, the only sister of Jim and Bill and their two brothers. Pearl was one of the first babies born in Banff. Phil became one of the park's first wardens in 1907 and later served as local magistrate. In the Canadian army he became a lieutenant-colonel. He and Pearl operated the CPR bungalow camp at Wapta Lake. Before she died in 1973, Pearl donated the family home and contents to the neighbouring Whyte Museum of the Canadian Rockies.

John F. Morrison (1860-1917) - He moved west to Manitoba from Bruce County, Ontario with his family at the age of twelve. Much of this trip was made by ox-cart. After working at farming and banking in North Dakota he came to Banff in 1913 and was appointed timber inspector.

Louis Samuel Mumford - He was born in Windsor, Nova Scotia. Mumford lived in Banff for thirty five years and was with the warden service from 1913 to 1921. In 1922 he was in charge of the campground at the Spray River. He died in Calgary in 1943 at the age of ninety three.

Mrs. Anna Mumford - She was a native of Falmouth, Nova Scotia. Anna was married to Louis for fifty four years. She spent thirty two years in Banff after moving from Innisfail. She was a very dedicated church and community worker. Anna died in 1933 at the age of seventy six.

Jack Naylor - He came to Canada from Ireland in 1914. After serving in World War I, he was employed as a park warden for thirty seven years and then spent eight years with the Department of Forestry. He died in 1965.

George Noble (1879-1965) - He was born in Woolwich, England and came to Canada in 1909. He operated a photographic business for his uncles, George and William Fear, who owned a curio business. In 1919 George bought the photo business and by 1932 acquired the remainder of the Fear Brothers' business. His wife was the sister of Ethel Peyto (Bill Peyto's second wife).

William (Bill) Noble (1877 or 1878-1951) - Bill was born in Woolwich, England. He came to Canada in 1910 to join his brother George who had emigrated the previous year. Prior to this, Bill had apprenticed with the Merchant Marines on an around the world trip. During the Boer War, he had served with the ordnance corps. When he first arrived in Banff, Bill worked as a cook for Billy Warren's outfitting business. In 1913-14 he spent a short time in the warden service. He then operated a shoe and harness repair shop on Banff Avenue before joining the government service. In World War I he went overseas with the 12th CMR Regiment. On his return he became caretaker of the Cave and Basin facility.

Lorne Orr - He was the manager of the King Edward Hotel for many years. He also operated a Dodge car dealership in Banff. Lorne died in 1955 at the age of seventy five. His father, Wesley Fletcher Orr, was a Calgary mayor.

Mrs. Anna May Orr - She was born in 1886 in Teeswater, Ontario. She came west with her parents as an infant to Field, B.C. Anna moved to Banff in 1916. She was very active in hospital work serving one year as president of the hospital auxiliary. Anna died in 1958.

Fred Pepper - He worked as a mechanic at the Luxton Garage. He also worked for the Department of Highways. In The Banff Crag & Canyon, he advertised himself as "The Automobile Doctor".

Ebenezer W. (Bill) Peyto (1869-1943) - Walter's older brother came to Canada from Kent, England in 1887. He began guiding with Tom Wilson in 1893 or 1894. In 1894 he crossed Bow Summit and explored the Mistaya Valley including the Peyto Lake area (named in his honour). One of Bill's early clients in 1895 was Walter Wilcox. Wilcox's 1896 book described Bill as efficient, daring, highly imaginative, an excellent man with horses and a good friend. Bill served in the Boer War. In 1901 he was the guide for the first successful ascent group on Mount Assiniboine (Swiss guides Christian Hasler and Christian Bohren and Rev. J. Outram). After his first wife, Emily, died in 1906, Bill spent a lot of time working on his mining and trapping interests in the area of Simpson Pass. He joined the warden service in 1911 before going overseas for World War I. He overcame serious war wounds and returned to the warden service working in the Healy Creek area. His cabin in Banff was named "Ain't It Hell".

Charlie V. Phillips - He joined the warden service in 1915 and served at Massive, Lake Louise and Field before moving to Jasper Park where he was supervising warden at the time of his retirement in 1952. Charlie died in Victoria in 1957 at the age of sixty nine.

Walter "Wattie" Potts - His father was William Potts, a partner of Frank Rigley who built the Park Hotel in Banff in 1902 on the site that was later the Cascade Hotel. Walter first guided for Brewsters. During World War I, while serving in the 12th Mounted, he was wounded in the field and taken prisoner. In World War II he served as a cook in the Calgary Highlanders. He died in 1957 at the age of sixty seven.

William J. Potts - This native of Montreal is listed in the "1911 and 1914 Wrigley's Directories" as a licensed guide. From 1929 to 1933 he was a warden in Banff National Park. From 1934 to 1940 he was a supervising warden in Banff.

Dr. Norman J. Quigley (1897-1970) - He graduated as a dentist in 1919. He practised in Banff for fifty years except for time away during World War I and World War II serving in the Dental Corps. His interest included sports, photography, painting and fishing.

James Reid (1873-1933) - He came to Banff in 1910 from Peterborough, Ontario. James operated the Reid Funeral Home for nineteen years. His wife was Edna (1874-1959).

Ralph Rink - He was from Sweden. He started working for Brewsters at Lake Louise in 1912. Later he became the Alpine Club outfitter. He and A.O. Wheeler operated a horse transport business under the name of Alpine Pack Train.

R.T. Rodd - He was the superintendent of the Fish Hatchery when it first opened. In 1917 he resigned his position to go overseas with the 7th Battery in World War I. He returned to Banff after the war. In 1924 he moved to Edmonton to work for the Department of Marine and Fisheries.

Carl Rungius (1869-1959) - He was born in a village that is now part of Berlin. He journeyed to North America in 1894 to visit an uncle in Brooklyn. He then spent most of the next ten years travelling the American west, hunting and painting. His first visit to the Banff area was in 1904. For many years, he returned to Banff each summer to take photos and sketch. He would then return to his New York studio to complete the paintings in the winter months.

Inspector Ryan - Mr. Ryan first came to Banff in 1908 and served as a corporal and sergeant for a number of years with the RNWMP. He returned to Banff as an inspector in 1919. He later served as a superintendent in Halifax and became deputy commissioner in Regina. He was seventy eight when he died in 1958.

Arthur Saddington - He was the Banff postmaster for forty six years before retiring to Victoria where he passed away in 1958.

Norman B. Sanson - He first came to Banff from Toronto in 1892. Prior to this he was a member of the Queen's Own Rifles during the Riel Rebellion. Sanson first worked as an accountant in Banff before he took over the position of curator of the Banff Museum in 1896. In addition to his extensive studies in wildlife, geology and fauna, one of his responsibilities was the operation of the weather observatory on top of Sulphur Mountain. In 1931 Norman was honoured for his 1000th ascent of the mountain. He joined the Alpine Club in 1913 and was the first president of the Skyline Hikers from 1933 to 1936. His home was at 110 Muskrat Street. He died in 1949.

Bert Sibbald - He was one of the original guides to work for the Brewsters. He and Billy Warren established the Banff Motor Co. His brother was Howard.

Howard E. Sibbald - (abbreviated in the journals to HES) Howard and his brother and sister came west from Barrie, Ontario with their parents in 1875 to the Morley area. His father, Andrew, was one of Alberta's pioneer school teachers. Howard spent his early working years on a ranch near Morley, as an Indian agent at Gleichen and then operating a store at Exshaw. He became Chief Warden of Rocky Mountains Park in 1905. When the Banff-Windermere Road opened in 1923, he was appointed Superintendent of Kootenay National Park until his retirement in 1928. He was well respected throughout his years of service as a warden. He died in 1938 at the age of seventy three.

Jimmy Simpson - He came to Canada in 1896 at the age of twenty two from Lincolnshire, England. He began his guiding career with Tom Wilson before starting his own business. In the winter, he spent his time trapping between Banff and Jasper. He guided Sir James Outram's expedition to the Columbia Icefields area where they made many first ascents. He became an accomplished artist and developed friendships with artists such as Carl Rungius. Jimmy built the well-known Num-Ti-Jah Lodge on the shores of Bow Lake. He died in 1972.

Jack Standly (1865-1943) - He moved from Grofton, Ontario to Prince Albert in 1882. Later he homesteaded in the Fort Macleod area. In the 1890s Jack worked in Banff as a carpenter for Dr. R.G. Brett. In 1898 he took part in a pack horse trip to the Yukon. On his return he ran a sightseeing boat operation at Lake Minnewanka where he earned the nickname "Captain Jack". He also built a small tourist chalet at Lake Minnewanka.

Annie Staple (1883-1973) - She came to Canada from England with her husband Tom in 1907. In 1916 she became the first permanent gatekeeper of the park. When the park boundaries moved eleven miles west in 1930 and the name changed to Banff National Park, she continued as the chief gatekeeper until her retirement in 1948.

Tom Staple - He was employed by the cement plant in the Exshaw area before becoming the first permanent warden for the area of Rocky Mountains Park near the east park gate.

E.E. Stewart - He worked as an accountant in the government office, retiring in 1924.

James Stewart (1883-1951) - He was born in Charleston, Nigg, Scotland and came to Montreal in 1903. In 1912 he moved to Strathmore prior to settling in Banff. He first worked as a teamster for the Brewster Company before joining the government service. In 1945 he was injured while operating a grader. After slipping on an icy street, he died after a short stay in hospital.

J. Stinson - He served as the assistant Chief Engineer of Canadian National Parks.

Edgar "Ted" Tabuteau - He came to Banff in 1898 from Ireland. He had served in the Boer War and at the age of seventeen had sailed around the world. He worked as a driver for both Dr. Brett and Norman Luxton. He worked for the parks department for twenty five years until his retirement in 1946. He was seventy one when he died in 1947.

Jack Thomas - He came to Banff in 1913 from Vernon, B.C. and started work with the Brewster Transport Co. He then ran his own livery stable on Bear Street on the site that became The Banff Crag & Canyon office. He retired in 1956 and died the following year.

Arthur Unwin - He was born in London and came to Canada in 1902, homesteading until 1905 at Hay Lake, Alberta before moving to Banff. Art, his brother Sid and sister Ethel started a guiding and packing business. They also established a boarding house called "Cozy Camp". Later Arthur ran a bakery business supplying Banff and Bankhead. After serving in World War I with the 22nd Battery, he was employed by Standish and Sons. By 1923 Arthur had started his own contracting and lumber business, expanding to include a hardware by 1926. Unwin's Ltd was incorporated in 1930 when the business took over the lumber yard of Skov Lumber Company. He was sixty six when he died in 1947.

Sid Unwin - He worked as a guide and outfitter in the Banff area. The Indians called him "Mustiyah Nahounga" or the running rabbit. After being part of the Mary Schaffer expedition to Maligne Lake in 1908, he had a mountain near the lake named in his honour He joined the 22nd Battery, 6th Howitzer Brigade for World War I, but was tragically killed overseas in 1917. His sister and friends had a stained glass window placed in St. George's in the Pines Anglican Church in his memory.

Sidney Vick - He spent some time in the Banff area as

Fisheries Inspector. He also had an interest in painting.

Dr. Charles D. Walcott - He was a famous researcher in geology and paleontology who spent a great deal of time in the Banff area. Dr. Walcott served for twenty years on the executive of the Smithsonian Institute. He died in 1927.

G.B. Ward (1887-1932) - He was a native of New Brunswick. He operated a business supplying coal and wood, saddle horses and draying. He helped build Fay Hut in 1926.

Sam Ward (1884-1973) - He came to Banff from London, England in 1912. In his job as a finishing carpenter he worked on many dwellings in Banff. He was also well known for his music hall recitations. He later moved to Victoria.

Stanley Ward - He worked for the Livery Stable Co.

William Ward - He came from London, England in 1902. He worked on the building of the Sulphur Mountain trail. After a few years in Summerland, B.C., he came to Banff in 1914 and served as the assistant postmaster until his retirement in 1938.

James M. Wardle (1888-1971) - He was superintendent of Rocky Mountains Park from 1918 till 1921 after the death of the previous superintendent, S.J. Clarke. Wardle had spent six years with the highway department. He then became Chief Engineer of Parks until 1935, succeeding Captain Grey. From 1935 till 1952 he worked at various appointments in Ottawa. His family was close friends with Carl Rungius.

Jack R. Warren (abbreviated in the journals as JRW) - After working as a park warden in Banff, Jack succeeded

Howard Sibbald as Chief Warden in Banff. His brother was Billy Warren, a Banff area guide and businessman, who married Mary Schaffer, the well known photographer, artist and writer.

A.E. Welby - He was born in Sollarton, Notts, England in 1889. He worked on railways in England and Uganda. After living one year in Mombasa, he returned to England. He also worked on railways in India and on railways and mining in Chile before coming to Canada. He became the CNR's divisional engineer between Jasper and Edson. In 1916 he joined the Canadian Engineers serving in Ypres. The Royal Engineers seconded him and he assumed the rank of Acting Major. After the war he joined the irrigation department of the Dominion Government. He spent ten years in the Banff area with the parks branch.

Dave White (1864-1940) - He was born in New Brunswick. Dave arrived in the Banff area in 1886 when Siding 29 was still in existence. He worked as a section foreman until 1894. That same year, he started "Park Store", a general store which his sister had to operate for six months while Dave journeyed east to take a business course. From 1904 to 1907 he and D.C. Bayne ran a store at Bankhead. Sam Armstrong worked with White during the time his business was known as Dave White and Co. (1908-1928). The business later became Dave White and Sons. This name is still visible on the façade of the old building on Banff Avenue.

Percy Williams - He came to Bankhead in 1913. Later he moved to Banff and operated a painting and decorating business with his son, Nelson. In 1916 he helped raise money to send cigarettes and tobacco overseas to soldiers. At this time he was working for CPR express.

James A. Wood - He was assistant superintendent in Rocky

Mountains Park before becoming superintendent of the park from 1921 to 1927. Later he was superintendent of Prince Albert and Jasper National Parks. He died in 1949.

Tex Wood (1882-1978) - He was most commonly known as Tex, although his complete name was Nello "Tex" Vernon Wood. He first came to Banff in about 1905/1906 and worked for Jim Brewster. For several years he accompanied Dr. Charles D. Walcott (the head of the Smithsonian Institute in Washington) and his wife Mary Vaux Walcott on their annual summer scientific field trips. Tex first joined the warden service in about 1915, patrolling the Sunshine area. After a number of years with the warden service, he started his own pack outfitting business. Later he worked for Kootenay National Park before retiring in B.C.

Ben Woodworth Jr. (1891-1956) - This son of Ben Sr. and Elizabeth Woodworth worked for the Dominion Government as a road builder.

Ben Woodworth Sr. (1861-1920) - He died while on duty as caretaker of the Buffalo Park after breaking his neck in a fall from his horse. He had moved to Banff in 1890 from Canning, Nova Scotia. His various jobs included foreman of the CPR stables, foreman of the Sanitarium stables for fifteen years, and two years on the trail working for Tom Wilson. After two or three years in Kootenay country he spent the final eight years of his life as the caretaker of the Buffalo Park. His daughter Annie married Ulysses La Casse.

Joe Woodworth (1892-1976) - This Banff native (son of Ben Sr.) first worked as a CPR messenger boy and as a bellhop at the Sanitarium Hotel, Grand View Villa and the Alberta Hotel. Later he became foreman of the Bretton Hall stables. From 1912 to 1915 he packed with Jimmy Simpson in the Kootenay Plains area. He was seriously wounded in

World War I and suffered the loss of an arm. After the war he worked as the townsite agent in charge of land and as building and plumbing inspector. From 1943 to 1953 he operated his own real estate and insurance business.

Percy "Beef" Woodworth - He was born in 1889 in Banff (a brother of Joe and Ben Jr.). He first worked as a printer's devil for The Banff Crag & Canyon. However, a strong interest in horses soon had him herding horses at the age of 17 for Jimmy Simpson. His first government work was at a forest fire on Wardle Creek in Kootenay Park in 1921. When he first started working as a warden at Clearwater, he lived for a year in a tent until the cabin was built. He also worked at the government ranch at Ya Ha Tinda, spent two years at Castle Mountain and a short time in Banff. Most of his many years as a warden were spent in the Lake Louise area.

Andrew S. "Scotty" Wright - He came to Alberta at the turn of the century from Sterling, Scotland. He lived in Crossfield, Cochrane, Canmore and Bankhead before moving to Banff. He was one of the first game wardens appointed. After seventeen years as a warden, Scotty took up mountain guiding and trapping. During World War II, he worked with the experimental section of the United States Army at the Columbia Icefield for which he was recognized with the rank of honorary sergeant. He died in 1960 at the age of seventy three.

Journal Entry from March 25th, 1916

Journal Entry from March 28th, 1916

NATIONAL PARKS OF CANADA
DEPARTMENT OF THE INTERIOR

Carry this diary with you—write it out at the end of each day's work.

Insert, daily, number of hours on duty. Mileage travelled.

Forward diary at the end of each month to the Superintendent of Park.

Show the route travelled by you on the map furnished by the Superintendent of Park and indicate thereon features of special interest, such as bodies of water, burned areas, etc.

Return this map to the Superintendent at the end of season.

Warden Diary instructions

Date...19........
Weather ....
Route travelled ....
....
No. of miles travelled ....
And how RR.........Auto.........Speeder.......Riding.........Boat ....Walking........
Fires seen—Number ....
        Location...
        Cause..
        Area burned ....
        Value (approx.)...
Names of persons met...
Guns sealed..
....
Any illegal acts discovered...
....

Warden Diary sample page

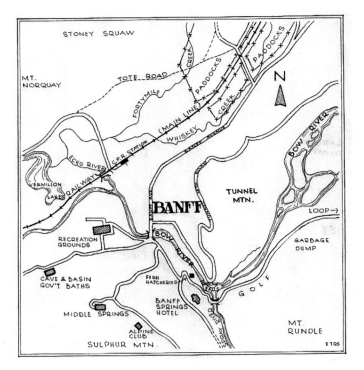

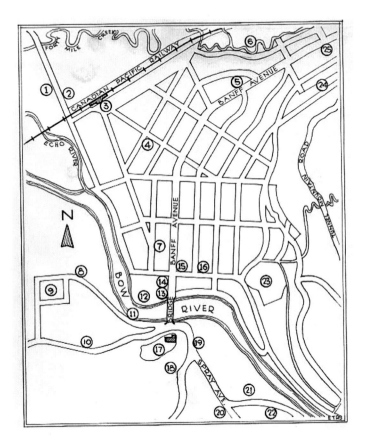

Legend for Map

1. Road to Vermilion Lakes and Lake Louise
2. Moffatt's Dairy
3. Banff Station
4. Government stables
5. Walter H. Peyto family home
6. Whiskey Creek
7. Government stores
8. Road to Recreation Grounds
9. Recreation Grounds
10. Road to Cave and Basin and Sundance Canyon
11. Boathouse
12. Zoo
13. Park Museum
14. RCMP
15. Rundle United Church
16. St. George's Anglican Church
17. Brett Sanitarium
18. Road to Alpine Club and Upper Hot Springs
19. Hospital
20. Road to Banff Springs Hotel
21. Fish Hatchery
22. Road to Golf Course, Garbage Dump and Loop Drive
23. Cemetery
24. Upper Road to Hoodoos and Anthracite
25. Road to Calgary

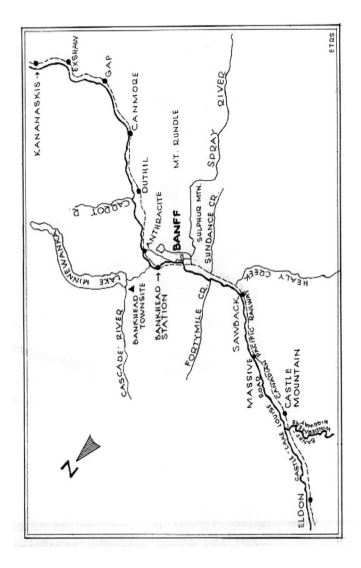